A FAITH FOR LIFE

A FAITH FOR LIFE

A LION BOOK
Tring · Belleville · Sydney

Acknowledgments

Andes Press Agency 53 (above left)
Barnaby's Picture Library 9, 16 (right), 26–27, 99, 126–127
Bildhuset 100 (above), 179 (below)
British Museum, London 140 (above right), 141 (below), 155
British Tourist Authority 166, 167 (below left)
John Callister 124 (above)
Camerapix Hutchison 5 (below), 11 (below), 13 (below left), 14, 15, 17 (centre left), 42, 44, 54–55, 56, 71 (below right), 77, 98, 103, 117 (below), 167 (above left), 178, 181
J Allan Cash 12 (above), 13 (right), 44–45
Central Press 125 (below)
Jonathan Chao 61 (below)
Church Missionary Society 17 (above left), 45, 95 (top), 106 (above), 111, 115, 125 (above), 163 (above), 164 (above), 167 (below right), 179 (above), 184–185, 187 (below)
Coventry Evening Telegraph 172–173
Paul Craven 117 (above right), 186 (both)
Daily Telegraph Colour Library / A Howarth 50–51 / GEG Germany 110
John Hessletine 143 / Adam Woolfitt 144 (below)
Tony Deane 48, 48–49
Fritz Fankhauser 8, 32, 41 (below), 60, 104–105, 129, 158–159, 185
FEBA 187 (above)
Format Photographers / Jenny Matthews 21 / Raïssa Page 91 / Maggie Murray 117 (top) / Brenda Prince 120
Sonia Halliday Photographs / Barry Searle 10, 12 (below) / Sonia Halliday 39 (top), 40, 49, 58 (all left), 59 (below left), 62–63, 64, 66–67, 72, 78–79, 80–81, 92 (all), 93 (all), 100 (below), 146–147, 164 (below) / Jamie Simson 43 / Jane Taylor 41 (above right), 47, 152–153 / FHC Birch 96 / Sister Daniel 87
Hodder & Stoughton 173 (below)
Michael Holford 169
Ikyrkans Internationella Av-Tjanst / Leif Gustavasson 36, 51, 71 (below left), 101 (above), 165 (above)
Peter Jennings 157
Keston College 53 (below left)
Frank W Lane / W Rohdich (below right) 4
Lion Publishing / David Alexander 38, 41, 108, 136–137, 138 (above) / Courtesy of Trustees of British Museum 140 (above left, below), 141 (above left and right), 147 / Haifa Maritime Museum, Israel 154 / Jennie Karrach 16 (left), 17 (below right), 102, 106 (below), 168, 174–175, 176–177 / Jon Willcocks 17 (below left), 70 (below), 71 (above right), 97, 116, 131 (left), 183
Phil Manning, with the help of Church's Ministry among the Jews 69
Mansell Collection 191 (left and right)
Grant Masom 101 (both below)
Open Doors 61 (above)

Brian Osborne, Lime Tree Studio 94–95, 161
Oxford Scientific Films 4 (below left)
Pictorial Press 26, 107
Picturepoint 108–109
Jean-Luc Ray 11 (above right), 13 (above left), 70 (above), 71 (centre), 134, 160, 162, 167 (above right), 188–189
John Rylands Library 39 (below)
Science Photo Library 3, 4 (centre left), 5 (above), 30–31, 130, 190
SCM 53 (above right), 191 (above)
Scottish Tourist Board 89
Doug Sewell 71 (above left), 86–87, 86, 164–165 (below)
Clifford Shirley 164–165 (above), 165 (below)
Peter Stiles 101 (centre)
Topham 74–75, 182
Peter Trainer / London City Mission 124 (below)
Dr Harold Turner 58 (above right)
UPI / CEN 53 (below right)
Woodmansterne 59 (above left), 167 (centre)
World Vision 135
Olav Wikse 163 (below)
Wycliffe Bible Translators 46, 156–157
ZEFA cover, 1, 4 (above both), 6, 10–11, 12–13, 17 (above right), 18–19, 20, 22, 24–25, 28, 28–29, 33, 34, 35, 36–37, 58 (below right), 59 (both right), 65, 68, 73, 76–77, 82–83, 84, 112–113, 117 (above left), 118, 118–119, 121, 122, 122–123 (all), 128, 131 (right), 138 (below), 142, 144 (above), 145, 148–149, 170–171, 171, 173 (above), 192

Published by
Lion Publishing plc
Icknield Way, Tring, Herts, England
ISBN 0 85648 578 0
Lion Publishing Corporation
10885 Textile Road, Belleville,
Michigan 48111, USA
ISBN 0 85648 578 0
Albatross Books
PO Box 320, Sutherland, NSW 2232
Australia
ISBN 0 08760 618 5

First edition 1985

Printed in Hong Kong

INTRODUCTION

What makes us tick? What do we base our lives on? What are the values and attitudes which make us choose to do one thing rather than another, or choose one style of life rather than another?

This book gives a picture of a living, world faith. Christianity has certain values, beliefs, patterns of life. It makes claims, offers promises.

It is important that we know what these claims are, whatever our own faith (and everyone believes something!). The Christian faith has been a key factor in the formation of the modern world. Today it is a key factor in many developing parts of the world. It is vital that we understand it, know what its beliefs are — and what they are not.

In words, pictures, quotations and stories, this book describes Christian belief, and it also tries to give a feel of what it means to be a Christian today. It is written from a committed viewpoint: but it is not just written for insiders, for the already committed. It is up to the reader to have the last word.

Each of the six sections starts with something we may know or see in the world around. What lies behind Christmas? What are all these people doing . . . ? This then leads into a description of six key areas of Christian belief. The sections are broken down into small units so that it is easy to see what is going on. *A Faith for Life* is also accompanied by a teacher's book with ideas and guidelines for discussion material.

CONTENTS

The Authors

The Rev. David Field BA is an author and lecturer in Ethics and New Testament Greek at Oak Hill Theological College, London.

Dr Myrtle Langley spent several years teaching in Kenya and lecturing at Trinity College, Bristol; she is now Diocesan Missioner in Liverpool.

Mags Law has a Master's degree in Educational Psychology. She taught in schools for some years before becoming a freelance writer. She also sings in a rock band.

The Rev. John Young BD MA has had wide experience in teaching and as head of an RE department. He is Chaplain of the College of Ripon and York St John and the author of several books.

David Day BA MEd MTheol is Lecturer in Religious Studies at the School of Education in the University of Durham.

THE WORLD ABOUT US

David Field

1

Crack!
The shell breaks.
A feeble, wet chick sees daylight for the first time.
It happens many times every day.
But the beginning of life never loses its fascination.
What came first — the chicken or the egg?

Right down through the ages, people have wondered and guessed how life on earth began. In our century, modern science has suggested a few answers.

● Some scientists believe that everything started with a 'big bang' — a huge explosion which started a long chain-reaction and finally brought life to Planet Earth.

● Other scientists say that we should talk about 'continuous creation' — there is no evidence of any dramatic beginning, so the universe must always have been there.

But these two suggestions do not answer our biggest questions:

● If everything began with a bang, what caused the bang?

● If the universe has always been there, how and why does it exist?

These are problems that science cannot tackle because science is based only on what can be observed. If we want answers, we must look for other evidence.

'In the beginning, God . . .'

That is Christianity's answer. It comes right at the beginning of the Bible. Before God, nothing at all existed. It was God who started everything off, by a word of command.

There is a big difference between the way God made the universe and the way people make things today. If you design and construct a model, someone may say, 'That's really creative!' But even if you did not buy a kit, you still had to find the materials to make the model. God was creative in a completely different way. He began with nothing.

When we read the Bible's story of creation, we learn one more important fact about the Creator — he was pleased with everything he created. Unlike us, there was nothing he created that he disliked and wanted to throw away. When it was all finished, 'God looked at everything he had made, and he was very pleased.'

If we believe in this kind of Creator it makes a big difference to the way we think about the world. Some religions teach that the material world is a hostile place. But Christianity takes a much more positive view. If God made the world and was pleased with it, we can enjoy it too.

'So God created human beings . . .'

The Bible tells us that after God the Creator made the world, he made people — man and woman. In many ways they were the same as the rest of creation. But, the Bible tells us, 'God created human beings, making them to be *like himself*.' Human beings are *different*, even though there are physical similarities with animals. So what makes human beings different from the rest of creation? Christians believe that there are three basic features of being human:

● **Human beings were made to live in a special relationship.** Animals mate and herd together for self-protection, but man and woman were made to belong together in a different way. The relationship between a man and a woman is special. God is love, and he made human beings to be like him in their lives together. Above all, human beings were specially created to have a close, loving relationship with God, their Creator.

● **The first human beings were told to live in a special way.** Only God is completely good, but every man and woman knows by instinct what living a good life is all about.

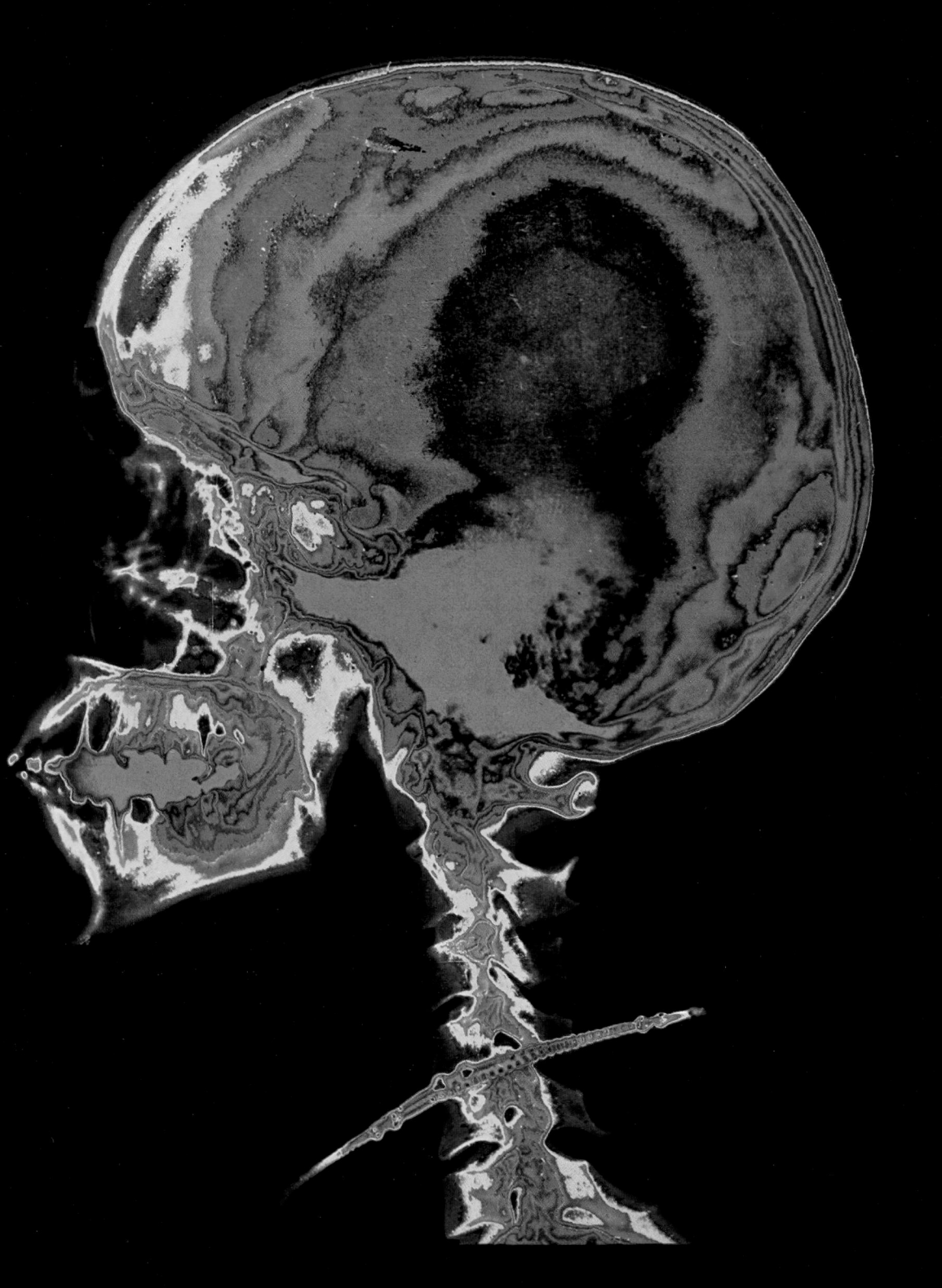

The natural world shows astonishing variety even in its smallest details. Here, a rhino beetle mimics the real thing.

Below Radiolaria are a type of plankton that live in the sea. Their skeletons are made of silica and are important in the formation of sedimentary rocks.

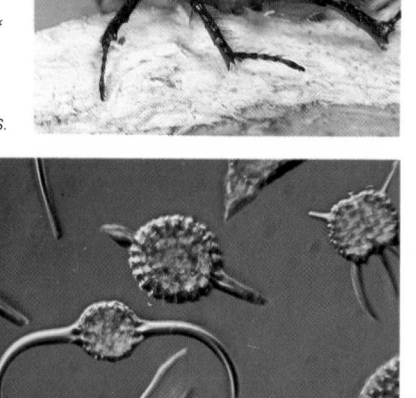

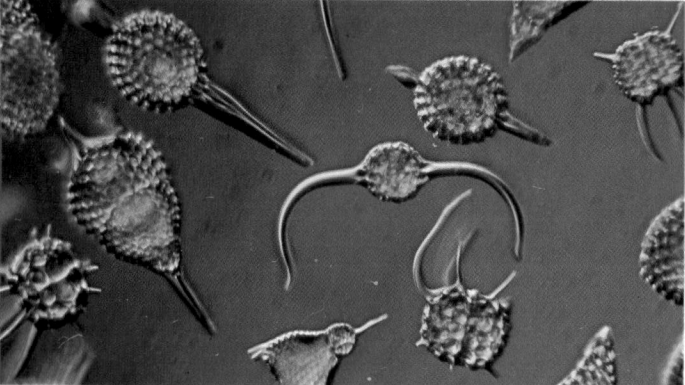

Above Anthias swim through the soft corals of the Red Sea.

Below The hummingbird beats its wings up to eighty times per second. It is able to hover motionless, and even fly backwards.

Right There are 2,600 species of frogs and toads today. This green toad can be found in most parts of Europe.

We all have consciences, though they can become warped. Our ability to tell right from wrong is another way in which we mirror the Creator.

● **Human beings were told to do a special job.** Man and woman were part of God's creation, but they were also told to look after it. They could not create in the same way as God, but they could — and still do — control and develop his creation.

This sounds all very well. But reading the first two chapters of the Bible is rather like looking at the universe through rose-tinted glasses. God may have been pleased with everything he made, but some very unpleasant things happen in his world. Volcanoes and earthquakes devastate and kill. Famine and disease destroy communities. And people who are made like him, the God of love, can behave in horribly unloving ways towards one another. Why?

'So the Lord God expelled him . . .'

Christianity does not ignore the dark side of the picture. In fact, it is the Christian faith which makes sense of both the good and the bad in the world. Most other religions, and ideologies such as Marxism, are not realistic about evil. Something very wrong has happened to the whole of creation, and the Bible traces it right back to a breakdown in human nature.

God did not create man and woman as senseless robots, pro-grammed to obey his commands without question. God allowed them to make their own choices and decisions. They were free to choose how to live — in the way God intended, or not.

The third chapter of the Bible

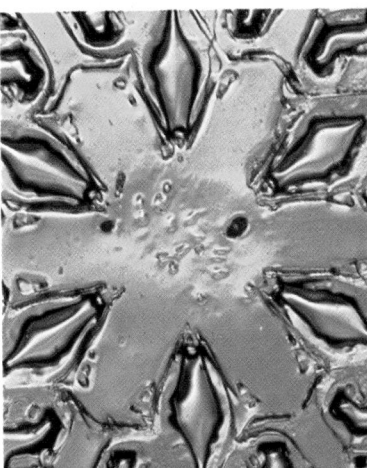

Left Snowflakes have six points and fall in their billions. But no two are the same.

Below The cheetah is said to be the fastest sprinter on earth, reaching speeds of up to 110 kph/68 mph in order to catch its prey. This speed is maintained by a remarkable flexing back and forth of the spine.

The Bible sees man and woman as the pinnacle of God's creation. But despite this special place, the human race has fallen and constantly goes wrong.

tells vividly how they made the wrong choice. Their deliberate disobedience to God did not just bring tragedy on their own heads. It affected the whole of the creation. Their sin (the Bible's word for it) was like a stone thrown into a pool. The ripples spread right across to the furthest bank.

The Bible explains that this sin, this rebellion against God, this selfishness, spoiled creation in three ways:

● **Sin brought conflict between human beings and their environment.** The human race and nature were meant to work together as partners. Sin made them into rivals — with nature only giving its produce reluctantly and people wasting and misusing the resources of nature.

● **Sin broke relationships between people.** Immediately, there was conflict between the sexes. Man tried to put the blame on woman for his act of disobedience. And throughout the Bible, we can find evidence of all the other break-downs in human relationships that tear the world apart today.

● **Sin broke the relationship between people and God.** This was the most serious breakdown of all. God banished man and woman from his presence. They could no longer be his friends. And they were quick to make God-substitutes to fill the emptiness left in their lives.

'God loved the world so much . . .'

If that was the end of the story, this book would never have been written. God might have left man and woman to live with the results of their disobedience. But the Christian gospel explains that he did not do so. Gospel means 'good news'. Sections 2 and 3 set out in more detail how God mounted his great rescue act, but the main facts are these:

● First, he prepared a nation in which men and women were his own 'chosen people'. They were to live by the standards he had set for them in his creation plan. This is the main theme of the Old Testament. God loved his people and promised to care for them and stand by them. His standards, his way of life, are laid out most clearly in the Ten Commandments. The people of Israel were taught very forcibly, too, how much they needed to be forgiven when they broke just one of these laws.

● Then came Jesus Christ. By his example he showed what it meant in practice to live up to God's standards. By his miracles he reversed the effects of sin, healing the sick and raising the dead. And by his own death and resurrection he made forgiveness possible. By taking the death penalty due to sinful people on himself, Jesus made a way to mend broken relationships between people and people, and between people and God.

● The final episode of the story has still to be written. The Bible forecasts that one day Jesus will come back to the world as its king, its chief, its liberator. His return will bring to an end all the misery that mankind's sin has caused. There will be no more suffering or death. And in some mysterious way, all the rest of creation will be re-made and every living thing join in the great victory celebrations. This is the hope that Christians have. It makes them optimists, even under the shadow of nuclear warfare and hatred between nations and peoples. Everything will be 'made new'.

But this is the point where we must step back from the future into the present, and take a closer look at the way people are made and the kind of lives they live.

For more about the claims made for the Bible, see Section 5, **God Speaks: The Bible.**

Man is nothing but:

FAT enough for seven bars of soap

IRON enough for one medium-sized nail

Sugar enough for seven cups of tea

Lime enough to whitewash one chicken coop

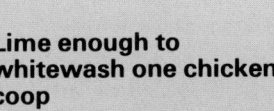

MAGNESIUM enough for one dose of salts

PHOSPHOROUS enough to tip two thousand two hundred matches

POTASH enough to explode one toy crane

SULPHUR enough to rid one dog of fleas.
Professor C.E.M. Joad

If you look at the chemicals in a human body, you will not find any startling new element. Like any animal, the first human beings needed to eat, drink and sleep.

The theory of evolution takes this similarity further — 'natural selection' ensures that the animals best suited to their environment survive. By this process of selection, the theory goes, it is possible to show that human beings and apes have developed from the same species. Some Christians see this theory of 'natural selection' as an attack on the Bible's account of creation. Others say it shows us how God created the world.

Is God like a machine-maker? Did he just set the universe going and then leave it to run itself? Some people believe he did. Others think he is part of the machine himself.

Christians belong to neither group. They believe God is quite separate from the universe. But they also believe he continues to rule its history and provide for its needs.

He does this in many ways:

● **By providing food.** One writer in the Bible said, 'All living things look hopefully to you, and you give them food when they need it' (Psalm 145:15).

A majority of the earth's population live in poverty. Why does God allow it?

● **By caring for animals and birds.** Jesus said, 'Not one sparrow is forgotten by God' (Luke 12:6).

● **By providing beauty.** 'Look at the field lilies', said Jesus. 'King Solomon in all his glory was not clothed as beautifully as they' (Matthew 6:28-29).

● **By providing for man's spiritual needs.** God reveals himself to people, answers their prayers, forgives them when they own up to their faults, and gives them power to live the right way. In the New Testament's words, 'Come near to God, and he will come near to you' (James 4:8).

● **By directing world events.** People are free to spoil anything that God provides. They can waste food, ruin beauty, ill-treat animals or refuse to pray. But they cannot stop him ruling the universe in his own way. When Jesus Christ came, he split history (see Galatians 4:4). And when Jesus returns, he is going to end it (see 1 Peter 1:3-9).

What is Sin?

'Sin' is a word that is easily misunderstood. Some people link it with serious crime or sexual immorality. They therefore get angry if they are called 'sinners'. In the Bible, sin is simply failing to keep God's standards. To sin is to break our relationship with God. The New Testament says, 'Everyone has sinned.' It uses five vivid words to describe what sin is:

● The first means 'missing the target'. Sin is failing to achieve the best, even when we aim at it.

● The second means 'stepping across'. A deliberate step across the dividing line between right and wrong is sin.

● The third means 'slipping across'. A slip of the tongue may be less deliberate than a clever lie, but it is still sin.

● The fourth means 'lawlessness'. Sin is knowing the law of God, and then defying it.
● The fifth means 'debt'. Sin is failing to pay to God the obedience which we owe him.

Shelving the blame

When you do something wrong these days it is the fashion to say, 'I couldn't help it. It's just the way I'm made.' Or, 'Don't blame me. Blame my parents and the way I was brought up.'

Jesus disagreed. He said that the root of our failures lies deep inside ourselves:

'It is what comes out of a person that makes him unclean. For from the inside, from a person's heart, come the evil ideas which lead him to do immoral things.'
Mark 7:20-21

Sin and suffering

If God is all-powerful and all-loving, why doesn't he stop suffering? Why does he allow children to die of malnutrition and people to get cancer? Christianity has no slick answers, but the Bible helps us to understand *why* there is suffering in God's world.

When God made the world, it was perfect and there was no suffering. But he made people free to choose between doing good and doing evil. Without that freedom, they would have been like robots.

But God's first people made a wrong choice and suffered terrible consequences. And through the ages generations have followed their bad example and reaped the same result. Most suffering today has a direct link with man's inhumanity to man.

The Bible teaches that this first 'fall' into sin has left a wound

which is still open. That is why many people suffer from handicaps and diseases which are no-one's fault today, least of all their own. Their personal tragedies are not God's punishment for their private sins, but the painful result of human error.

This is also why natural disasters like floods and earthquakes happen. Human sin upset creation's harmony. It spoiled man's environment as well as his private life. We cannot see where all of the links are, but there is a chain which connects mankind's sin with all the world's suffering.

Putting sin into reverse

Jesus came to reverse sin's effects. Using key words from the Old Testament, he declared that a whole new creation was beginning with himself:

'The Spirit of the Lord is upon me, because he has chosen me to bring good news to the poor. He has sent me to proclaim liberty to the captives and recovery of sight to the blind; to set free the oppressed and announce that the time has come when the Lord will save his people.'
Luke 4:18-19

Most human suffering has its roots in the evil people do to each other. There are slums in New Delhi because of the greed and indifference of other people.

Wherever we live, we are constantly reminded that the world is a small place. International airports offer fast travel to far-away places. Shops sell unfamiliar food for us to try. Turn the tuning knob on the radio, and you hear snatches of conversation in many different languages.

All this variety makes life much more interesting. Unfortunately, it creates big problems too. In today's 'global village' people of many different races and cultures are thrown together. In areas where there is a mixture of races, misunderstandings and fear can easily grow. People of different races find it hard to get work, except jobs that no one else wants. Some even have trouble in finding anywhere to live, unless they can pay very high rents. Throwing people of different races and cultures together can increase hostility — as well as increasing understanding.

Christians have their own explanations for differences of race and colour. And their faith also tells them what to do when people are treated unfairly because of their racial differences.

From the very beginning of our lives, human relationships are important. God has made us to enjoy friendships and to belong with other people.

Equality

First, **all people have equal value**. In the apostle Paul's words, 'From one man God created all races of mankind.' And the story of creation at the beginning of the Bible says, 'God created human beings, making them to be like himself.' In other words, people of all races are absolutely equal in God the Creator's sight, whatever the colour of their skins.

Some people like to trace their family tree back as far as they can go. They feel quite proud if they find that their great-great-grandfather was somebody

International travel has brought once-distant cultures into close contact with each other.

Differences matter

Second, **differences of race and culture are important**. The New Testament says that God is in charge of all history and geography: 'He himself fixed beforehand the exact times and the limits of the places where people would live.' People from different parts of the world have different customs, as well as skins of different colours, because their Creator meant them to be that way.

famous. But there is nothing to be proud about if the top of everyone's family tree looks exactly the same. And no one can ever look down on anyone else if everybody has been made by God like himself.

The Bible's picture of heaven confirms this. Standing before God's throne will be people 'from every race, tribe, nation, and language . . .' Whatever proud words people have written on their tomb-stones, there will be no racial discrimination in the life after death.

God's Mistakes?

The Bible's account of creation describes people of all races as equal. That contrasts with the flavour of some other creation stories.

A Hindu myth, for example, labels white and black skinned races as God's accidents. God made man of clay, the story goes, and put him in the oven. First, he over-estimated the time needed for baking, so his creation came out black and overdone. Next he under-estimated, which produced an undercooked white man. It was only on his third attempt that the Creator got it right — as all brown-skinned people demonstrate!

Jesus and Racism

There was no colour bar in Bible times. But there was harsh friction between people of different racial and cultural groups. In particular, no love was lost between Jews and Samaritans. A good Jew would accept no favours from a despised Samaritan. This gave Jesus' famous story about the Good Samaritan its main point — that God's love can break down all racist barriers. And the challenge at the end of the story was very direct. '*You* go, then', he told his listeners, 'and do the same.'

Peter and Racism

The apostle Peter was a racist, born and bred. As a strict Jew he would have nothing to do with non-Jews (Gentiles). It took a vivid dream to convince him that there are no racial barriers in God's kingdom.

Luke describes the details in chapter 10 of the Book of Acts. The end of the story finds Peter standing in a Gentile home and telling people about his change of heart:

'You yourselves know very well that a Jew is not allowed by his religion to visit or associate with Gentiles . . . I now realize that it is true that God treats everyone on the same basis. Whoever worships him and does what is right is acceptable to him, no matter what race he belongs to'
(Acts 10:28,34-35).

God wants people of different races to mix. He is in favour of emigration and immigration. But he wants immigrants to bring their various customs with them. He intends men and women from different racial backgrounds to share their music, their styles of dress and their favourite foods, not to lose them. It is rather like using all the different colours from a paint-box to make a brilliant picture, instead of mixing them all up together into a mucky mess.

No enemies

Third, **it is wrong to turn racial differences into divisions**. As we saw earlier, God's perfect world was spoiled by human selfishness. When groups of people act selfishly, they make enemies.

We see that happening in football crowds, when one set of supporters stop shouting for their own team and start throwing missiles at the other team's fans. Sadly, the same thing often happens when people of different races meet. If a family with black faces moves into a house, all their white neighbours may band together to keep other immigrants out. They are afraid that the value of their own homes will fall, and so hatred and violence are born.

The Bible teaches that minority groups in the community must be cared for and looked after, not rejected. 'Do not ill-treat foreigners who are living in your land', says the Old Testament; 'love them as you love yourselves.' Christian love is not just a nice feeling. It stands for practical action. It means supporting minority groups when they are attacked, challenging prejudice wherever it appears, and working hard to help multi-racial communities live and work together, to be integrated.

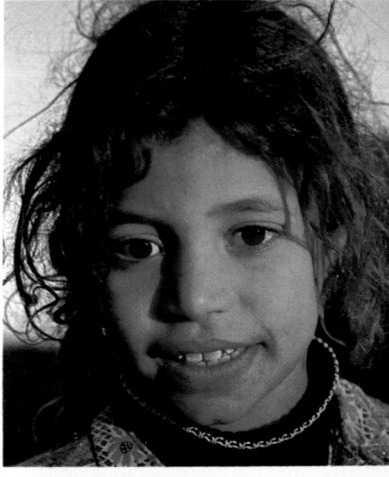

When Jesus came into the world, he put this Bible teaching into practice. He made his fellow-Jews very angry by the generous way he treated foreigners. And one of his purposes in dying on the cross was to reconcile people of different races. That explains why Christians try so hard to build bridges across divisions of race and colour today.

This cafe in Thailand does not serve hamburgers! But its different way of doing things shows the rich variety of human cultures.

From the moment we are born (and even before that), our sex is fixed. The physical differences between being a girl and being a boy seem very small at first. But then, as the years pass by and our bodies begin to grow, those differences become more obvious, more interesting and more important.

In the very first book of the Bible we are told that God himself made man and woman the way they are. And he did not regret it. 'He looked at everything he had made, and he was very pleased.'

Marriage is common all over the world, regardless of religion. This wedding took place in China.

Why did God arrange things this way? The Bible's account of creation gives us two answers.

Relationships

In junior school playgrounds groups of young girls often stand and talk well away from gangs of boys. They dress differently, play different games and find different things interesting. But that, as we know, is only a passing phase. Before long, boy and girl friend-ships deepen, couples pair off, and eventually marriages are made.

This is exactly how God planned it in the beginning. 'It is not good for man to live alone', he said. So he made woman, to end man's loneliness. And man quickly under-stood what his Creator had done. 'This is now bone of my bones and flesh of my flesh', he exclaimed, as he discovered someone of the opposite sex for the first time. By inventing sex, God had brought the warmth of deep personal relation-ships into human life.

Marriage is a relationship of a very special kind. The way couples get married varies from culture to culture. In some parts of the world, parents arrange their children's marriages for them. Elsewhere, young couples fall in love and marry, whether their parents approve or not. Wedding ceremonies differ enormously, too. But in spite of all the variations, there are three special features which mark off all marriages as something special.

Again, we find these three things spelled out in the book of Genesis.
● First, the man and the woman must promise to **stay faithful** to each other for life.
● Second, their promise must be **witnessed by others**. Society recognizes that they have made a new home together.

● Third, that promise must be sealed by the special act of togetherness which we call sexual intercourse, and which the Bible describes much more vividly as **'becoming one flesh'**.

That is what marriage means, however it is arranged.

Family life

God had a second purpose in creating man and woman as sexual beings. He told them, 'Have many children, so that your descendants will live all over the earth and bring it under their control.'

The arrival of a baby brings extra happiness into a married couple's life. That is just as much part of their Creator's design as the private closeness they enjoy in each other's arms. In fact, it is an exciting extension of that closeness. Children grow up in the warmth and security of their parents' love, until it is time for them to make special relationships of their own. It is all part of God's plan.

Today, there is a great deal of talk about 'family planning'. Limiting the size of families is certainly a right thing to do, if God's command to 'bring the earth under control' is taken seriously. Some parts of the world are getting out of control simply because there are too many mouths to feed. Nevertheless, our worries about world overcrowding must never make us despise the family. Getting married and bringing up children are two of the most rewarding things to do in human life, as God has designed it.

This is why Christians defend the values of *personal relationship* and *family life*. In many parts of the world those values are under attack. That is why Christians are often heard protesting against some

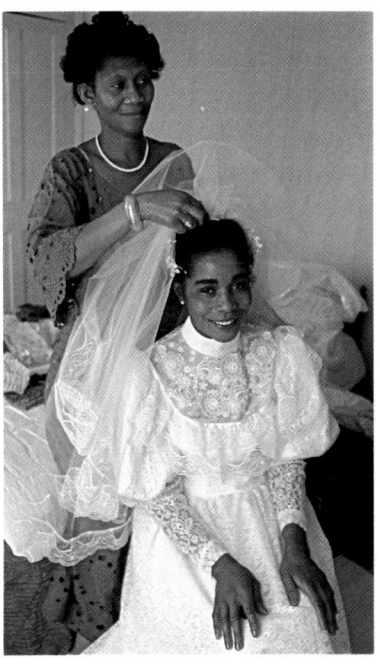

Most brides dress in a special way for their wedding day. Here a friend arranges the veil for a Ghanaian bride.

For more discussion about family relationships and about sex, see section 4, **A Faith for Living**.

social trends.

Christians are against pornography and prostitution, because they believe that sex is at its best in a relationship.

Christians are against divorce, not because they want people to live for ever in misery, but because divorce breaks up family life — and family life is worth protecting.

They are against a man and a woman living together without getting married because those who live in this way do not have that loving, long-term commitment. Nor do they experience the security and social recognition which are found in marriage.

Sex discrimination

In many parts of the world today, women suffer discrimination. It was no different in the days when Jesus lived. Every morning an orthodox Jew would thank God he had not been born a Gentile, a slave — or a woman!

Jesus' own attitude to women was revolutionary. He started a conversation with a woman by a well. He accepted women warmly among his disciples. And he taught in the temple's Court of Women, showing that he believed women were just as intelligent as men.

Paul the apostle echoed Jesus when he wrote, 'There is no difference . . . between men and women; you are all one in union with Christ Jesus.'

A church wedding before the confetti explosion.

Above *A Portuguese bride in traditional dress.*

Right *This bride from Laos displays her 'dowry' – wealth provided by her father to give her husband. Dowries are still given in many non-Western cultures.*

What is Marriage?

Jesus and Paul both turned to the Old Testament for a definition of marriage. The verse they used is Genesis 2:24:
'For this reason a man will *leave* his father and mother and *be united* to his wife, and they will become *one flesh*.'
The words in italics highlight the main features of marriage.
● **Leaving** father and mother was a great ceremony in Bible times. All the family, friends and neighbours took part. It was like having witnesses sign the marriage register at a wedding today — only it took much longer!
● **Being united** is the expression the Bible uses for a very close relationship. It stands for loyalty and lasting commitment.
● **Becoming one flesh** means not only having sexual intercourse, but also sharing all life's experiences — the pains and disappointments, as well as the joys and pleasures.

Christians believe that having sexual intercourse when you are not married is wrong. Apart from the risks of catching a disease or starting a baby, the main reasons for this ban are:
● The Bible says 'no'.
● Sex is more than an appetite. Animals have intercourse to satisfy themselves, but God's purpose for human sexuality is bigger than that.
● Having sex just for personal satisfaction is selfish. It degrades your partner.

● Sexual intercourse is meant to seal a relationship which is special to the couple and which will last for the whole of life.
● Having intercourse before getting married can actually undermine a good relationship.
● It is a lie to say that a person cannot know what love is all about until he or she has had sexual intercourse.

Left A bride from Pakistan.

Below An Israeli Yemenite bride shows her rings to a wedding guest.

Making love

The Song of Solomon is in the Old Testament. As these verses from the Song show, the Bible is rich in the joy of making love.

He says to her: 'How beautiful you are, my love! How your eyes shine with love behind your veil . . . Your lips are like a scarlet ribbon; how lovely they are when you speak. How beautiful you are, my love; how perfect you are! Your love delights me, my sweetheart and bride.'

She says about him: 'Promise me, women of Jerusalem, that if you find my lover, you will tell him I am weak from passion. My love is handsome and strong; he is one in ten thousand. His face is bronzed and smooth; his hair is wavy, black as a raven. His mouth is sweet to kiss; everything about him enchants me. My lover is mine, and I am his.'

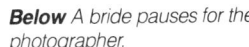

Below A bride pauses for the photographer.

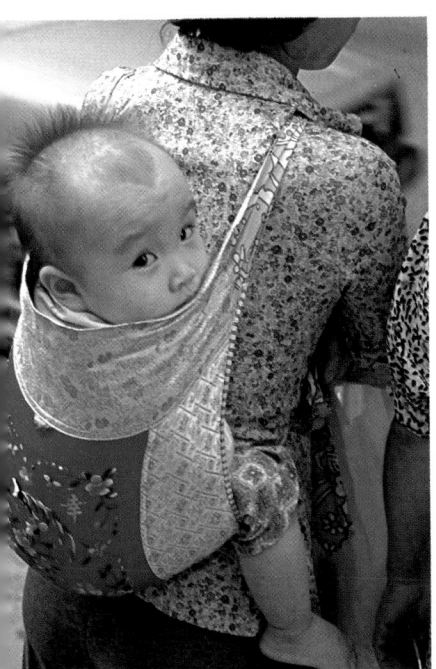

1.5 GOD'S WORLD — OUR WORLD

Today, in the western world, one of the more popular church services of the year is harvest thanksgiving. It is a special occasion when Christians stop to remember how much we rely on the world around us, and to thank God for providing us with our food.

It is easy to take nature for granted, especially if you live in a big town or city. People who buy their food in cans and plastic bags do not worry very much about a severe drought or a hard winter. But those who live in rural areas take these things much more seriously. They know that human life depends on things beyond our control, such as the seasons and the weather.

Jesus taught his followers to depend on God. He taught them to pray, 'Give us today our daily bread'. That prayer, still used regularly by millions of people, reminds us that all the world's resources belong to God. He is the Creator. He has made everything we see around us — not only the things we eat, but the things we wear, the scenery we enjoy and all the natural resources we use.

That belief makes Christians look at the world of nature in a special way. In practice, it means four important things.

We must treat nature with respect

If God created everything, all animals, birds and plants are our fellow-creatures. We are all part of the same big creation family. The fact that God has made trees and pigs, for example, means that they have their own special value and dignity, which foresters and farmers must always respect.

Jesus showed what this meant when he talked about shepherds

Christian Aid

Faith in Jesus is practical. Christians have always taken the lead in aiding the poor. Two glimpses of Christian action, ancient and modern, illustrate this.

● In the year 325, the historian Eusebius described how Christians went into action during a plague:

'Christians showed themselves at that time to all the heathen in the most brilliant light; for the Christians were the only people who, in the midst of so much and so great tribulation, proved by deeds their sympathy and love. Some busied themselves day after day with the care and burial of dead bodies (they were without number, and no one else bothered about them); others gathered together into one place all who were tortured by hunger and supplied them with food. When this became known, people glorified the God of the Christians, and confessed that they alone were the truly pious and God-fearing people, because they gave proof of it by their deeds.'

● In 1965, pop singer Cliff Richard became a Christian. Since then he has become deeply involved in the work of a world-wide relief agency called Tear Fund. He travels to places where people are in special need, to publicize their plight.

Human beings are God's creatures. Yet God has made us the managers of all creation. A famous Old Testament psalm highlights the contrast between the tininess and the greatness of the human race.

'When I look at the sky, which you have made, at the moon and the stars, which you set in their places — what is man, that you think of him; mere man, that you care for him?

Yet you made him inferior only to yourself; you crowned him with glory and honour. You appointed him ruler over everything you made; you placed him over all creation' (Psalm 8:3-6).

and sheep. A good shepherd, he said, is not just in the job for the money. He cares for his animals, and even gives them names. He risks his life for them when they are in danger. He knows when just one goes missing, even though he has dozens of others to look after.

We must manage nature

Some eastern religions teach that all life is sacred, so it is wrong for people to kill any animals to feed themselves or even to protect their health. Jesus never taught that. He told his followers that the lives of people are much more valuable than the lives of animals and birds — even though those are precious too.

In the Bible's description of creation, God made man and woman to be managers of all he had made. 'Bring it under your control,' he told them. 'I am putting you in charge.' If you have a garden, but do not look after it, then it soon gets full of weeds and out of control. It's the same with

nature. By careful farming, scientific research and technological development, we must manage God's world well.

We must use resources carefully

No good manager will waste his resources. He will make sure that everything is used at the right time and in the best way, with as little waste as possible.

That is why Christians are often to be found involved in conservation schemes. Re-cycling things like water, paper and glass is good management. Using a bigger car than you need (to impress the neighbours, perhaps) is bad management, because it wastes the precious supplies of fuel oil which the Creator has provided.

We must distribute resources fairly

We live in an unfair world. Rich nations make up only one-quarter of the world's population, but they get four-fifths of the world's income. In a typical year, twelve million children under the age of five die of starvation or malnutrition in the poorer countries, while their richer neighbours spend fortunes on slimming aids.

Jesus taught that God is on the side of the poor; and that he will punish those who do not share their resources with the hungry, the poor, the lonely, the sick and the cold. In his famous story of the Good Samaritan, he made it clear that 'loving your neighbour' means using the things you have to help those who are in greater need.

Are cars worth it? The lead in petrol fumes causes brain damage in young children, makes city air foul and contributes to the acid rain that destroys forests and lake life.

Technology's side-effects

Modern technology has some unpleasant side-effects.

● The use of nuclear fuel to produce energy is attractive. But what is to be done with the dangerous waste materials the process produces?

● The River Rhine flows through many countries in Europe. In 1969 forty million fish died in its waters. Industrial pollution was to blame.

Left Our eating habits greatly affect other living creatures. Where is the borderline between cruelty to animals and the legitimate use of them in feeding ourselves?

1.6 BOTH WORK AND LEISURE?

Motivation

What stimulates people to work hardest?
   Money?
   Promotion?
   Security?
   Job-satisfaction?
   Over and above these, Christians have an extra incentive:
'Whatever you do, work at it with all your heart, as though you were working for the Lord and not for men' (Colossians 3:23).

Breakdown

The Bible lists many ways in which sin spoils work relationships, among them:
● **Cheating the customer:**
'In the houses of evil men are treasures which they got dishonestly. They use false measures, a thing that I hate. How can I forgive men who use false scales and weights?' (Micah 6:10-11).
● **Cheating the worker:**
'Doomed is the man who builds his house by injustice and enlarges it by dishonesty; who makes his countrymen work for nothing and does not pay their wages' (Jeremiah 22:13).
● **Cheating the employer:**
'Slaves, obey your human masters with fear and trembling; and do it with a sincere heart, as though you were serving Christ. Do this not only when they are watching you, because you want to gain their approval . (Ephesians 6:5-6).

The Bible sees work as an important activity, whether it is paid employment or an unpaid 'labour of love'.

Some people live for their work. It is hard to get them to stop in the middle of a job, even for a meal. But most of us are not quite like that. When the demands of home-work clash with a party invitation, there is little doubt which we would rather do, given the choice. We may not actually *hate* our work, but we certainly look forward to the times when we are free to enjoy our leisure time.

The Bible has quite a lot to say about the balance of work and leisure in a person's life. It helps the Christian to see that both are valuable.

Work

God designed man and woman to be workers. That is the clear message which comes through the story of creation in the book of Genesis. He gave them *both* (not just the man!) firm instructions to rule and look after the world on his behalf and to use its resources for good.

Some of the jobs we do may not seem so grand or exciting as that, but everything we call 'work' today is really to do with managing a small corner of God's world. And 'work' means all sorts of jobs, not just what people are paid to do. Tidying a bedroom comes under that heading, just as much as setting up a new experiment in the chemistry laboratory.

God led the way by his own example. In most of the world's religions, work is beneath the dignity of the supreme deity or god. But the God of the Bible is different. Jesus himself said, 'My Father is always at his work to this very day.' One writer of the psalms describes him as the God who works with his hands like a manual labourer: 'The skies proclaim the work of his hands.' And he sends out his orders just like a modern executive sitting at his office desk: 'By the word of the Lord were the heavens made. He commanded, they were created.'

This is why Christians are among those who fight hard against unemployment. They believe that work is part of what it means to be human, and so to be out of a paid job spells the loss of something far more personal and precious than a pay-packet.

FILE

JOB

Unemployment

Work sometimes seems dull and boring. But life without work can be much more frustrating. A sociologist who conducted a survey among the jobless found the following reactions to unemployment.

● 'It's like somebody cutting your throat' (a 46-year-old man).

● 'I'm just occupying myself because it's so boring — unemployment is a down-hearted thing — there is nothing to do all day long' (a 25-year-old woman).

● 'You feel like a bit of a sponger' (a 23-year-old man).

● 'You find yourself getting up later and later. It comes on after a while — you know there's nothing to do, so you stay in bed most of the time' (a 19-year-old man).

Direction in life

Christians believe God has a purpose in life for everybody. In Paul the apostle's words, 'God has made us what we are, and in our union with Christ Jesus he has created us for a life of good deeds, which he has already prepared for us to do.'

In practice, this means:
● All my talents are God's gifts. He has equipped me to do something in life, even if I think I have no talents at all.
● A paid job is only part of what it means to have a direction in life. God's plan stretches from one end of my life to the other. It includes leisure time as well as working hours.
● My main ambition is to use my talents to serve God and other people. The question I ask myself as I face life is not 'How can I do best for myself?' but 'How can I put what I have been given to the best possible use?'

For more discussion about work, see section 4, **A Faith for Living**.

Leisure

Although God set a very high value on work, he did not want men and women to work every day of the week and have no time for anything else. Again, he set the example himself. After his work of creation, he rested — and one of the words the Bible uses for 'rest' means 'get your breath back'.

In the Ten Commandments, God ordered his people to follow his example. Every seventh day was to be a 'sabbath', a day kept free from work. Many Christians think of Sunday as the sabbath day, and treat it mainly as a day for worship. But in Bible times the idea of the sabbath took in much more than that.

The key idea was 'change'. All working people need a regular change from their jobs. That certainly includes the need to find proper time for worship (because it can so easily get squeezed out on a working day). But 'keeping the sabbath' also means finding opportunities to relax and enjoy all sorts of different leisure pursuits. Jesus annoyed the religious leaders of his time by ignoring the trivial details of their sabbath law. But he was also very careful to keep the valuable principle behind it, by giving his disciples regular breaks for rest and relaxation. Even they needed a change from time to time.

So both work and leisure have their own special value. The secret lies in striking a right balance between the two. The Bible suggests a mixture of six parts work to one part leisure. That is not meant to be a rule which must be slavishly obeyed, but it makes a very useful guideline.

Whoops!

1.7 GOOD AND EVIL

God is completely good, through and through. In Jesus' words, 'No one is good, but God alone.'

This means that every person who has ever lived shares something of God's good nature. No one is perfect, but every human being has an idea of what being perfect would be like.

In an ordinary family, sons and daughters often look like their parents. No child is an exact copy of his father or mother, but you can see the family likeness in the shape of a nose, the twist of a mouth or the build of a body. In some ways it is the same with God the Creator and the whole family of mankind. Everyone knows the difference between good and bad because God has made us all like himself.

Men and women generally have a sense of right and wrong. Children do, too. If someone gets punished for something he did not do, everyone shouts 'That's not fair!' If soldiers massacre an innocent crowd in one country, people all over the world are outraged.

Where do we get these strong feelings from? The way we are brought up has a lot to do with it. If we grow up believing that everyone should tell the truth, it may be because our parents punished us for telling lies when we were very small. If we are against violence, as adults, it may be because playground bullies were severely punished in the schools we went to when we were young.

The way we are brought up affects us for life. But the Bible tells us that human knowledge of good and evil has even deeper roots. It has more to do with the way we are *made* than with the way we are *educated*.

God's nature

When God made man and woman, he said, 'They will be like us'. And

The New Testament says that God's moral law is written on every person's heart. The United Nations' *Universal Declaration of Human Rights* is evidence that a common sense of right and wrong exists, shared by all human beings, whatever their culture or creed. Jacques Maritain, a member of the UNO committee responsible for the *Declaration*, was asked how the delegates could agree on human rights when they disagreed about most other things. 'We agree about the rights', he replied, 'but on condition that no one asks us why!'

In the New Testament, in the letter to the Romans, Paul puts the same thing in a different way. All human beings have a sense of right and wrong, he says, because God's law is 'written in their hearts'. We do not really have to be told that telling the truth is right. We do not actually need a school rule which says, 'It is wrong to cheat'. We know that sort of thing already by instinct, deep down inside ourselves, because it is part of being human.

God's law

Why then do we need school rules at all? If everyone knows the difference between right and wrong, why do people need laws to tell them the same things all over again? And if God made all human beings like himself, why do criminals exist?

The answers to questions like these point us towards the darker side of the Bible's creation story. God gave man and woman instructions about how to live. But he also allowed them to make their own decisions. They quickly rebelled against God. And when that happened, their sense of right and wrong became blurred. They could

Right and Wrong

It is a common belief that something is only wrong if you get caught doing it. As one politician put it, when the secrets of his sex life were exposed, 'There is a world of difference in doing something and not being found out, and doing something and being found out.'

Jesus disagreed. He taught that even the hidden things we do in the secrecy of our imaginations are wrong if they break God's moral law. He told his followers, 'Anyone who even looks at a woman with lust in his eye has already committed adultery with her in his heart.'

Christians believe they are promised special resources for living a good life:

● **God's pardon:** 'If we confess our sins to him, he can be depended on to forgive us and to cleanse us from every wrong' (John's words, in 1 John 1:9).

● **God's power:** 'God is always at work in you, to make you willing and able to obey his own purpose' (Paul's words, in Philippians 2:13).

Riot police in Germany enforce the rule of law at a demonstration.

Conscience

Everyone has a conscience. It is the name we give to the warning signals we get when we are about to do something wrong, and the guilt we feel afterwards if we have ignored the warning.

Conscience can usually be trusted, but we need to take care.

● **Conscience is not always God's voice.** Conscience is like a mirror. It reflects back to us the beliefs and standards we have taken on board earlier in life. If those standards are Christian, conscience will remind us of God's will. But the opposite is true as well.

● **Conscience needs educating.** Conscience is like a reservoir. It needs constant supplies of moral information if it is to give us reliable guidance. For Christians, this means a deliberate attempt to fill the mind with fresh knowledge about God's will.

● **Conscience can be silenced.** Conscience is like an opponent in the boxing ring. Hit it hard and often enough and it will be too weak to hit back. Tell a lie once, and conscience will jab you hard. Tell a thousand lies, and it will not even prick. A person's silent conscience does not necessarily mean he is in the right.

Love is the key to Christian living. Jesus said:
'Love the Lord your God with all your heart, with all your soul, with all your mind, and with all your strength.'
'Love your neighbour as you love yourself.'

still see the difference between good and evil most of the time, but it was like peering through a fog. Even worse, doing wrong became more attractive than doing right.

Today we all live in that fog, and we are all tempted to do the wrong things instead of the right. That is why we need laws and the police. It is also why God gave his people the Ten Commandments. They act as a torch to light up our choices between good and evil, and jolt our consciences when we give way to temptation.

God's Son

Jesus did three things to give back this clear sense of right and wrong

to people. And he also offered them help to do the right things.

● First of all, he lived a perfect life himself. When people looked at Jesus they saw something that rules and laws could never show them — real, lived-out goodness in a human being.

● Second, when he died, Jesus opened up the way for people to be pardoned by God for their moral failures. The New Testament calls it 'forgiveness of sins' and says that everyone who is genuinely sorry can find it, by putting their faith in him.

Many people begin to learn right from wrong through their parents or as members of a family.

● And third, after his resurrection, Jesus provided the power of his Spirit to help people break bad habits and show God's nature more clearly in their lives.

Christians do not claim to be perfect. But they do believe they have God's strength to overcome their weaknesses.

Which is the right way to go? In the complex decisions and problems of life we need clear guidance. Christians believe that the Bible can help us to take the best route.

Beyond the normal

Some people play occult games for fun. Christians have more respect and fear for supernatural powers than that. The Bible's advice is, 'Don't dabble'. There is evidence that at least some strange experiences of 'the paranormal' are genuine. Here are one or two things that baffle the scientists:

● **Clairvoyance.** Some people have the ability to 'see' things — in the past, present or future — which are invisible to others.

● **Levitation.** This is the power to make a person or thing rise from the ground and hover in the air, without support of any kind.

● **Psychokinesis.** The power of the mind to affect other people and objects.

● **Teleportation.** Some people apparently have the power to take themselves from one place to another without using any kind of transport.

Evil spirits

The Devil is alive and real! Jesus certainly thought so. He fought many hard battles against hostile supernatural powers. Once, after dramatically healing a boy who was in the grip of an evil spirit, he told those round him, 'Only prayer can drive this kind out, nothing else can.'

The Holy Spirit

Christians are sure that the Holy Spirit lives in every believer. 'You know him,' Jesus told his first followers, 'because he remains with you and is in you.' It is the Holy Spirit who gives a Christian power to live the kind of life that pleases God.

Wherever you travel in the world, you will find evidence of religion. Belief in the supernatural lies very deep in human nature. People everywhere search for something or someone to give their lives meaning and purpose. This something or someone is found beyond the range of the things people can see, hear or touch.

In some parts of the world it seems that religion is dying. In many countries of the western world the number of people who go to church is falling. Some people feel that in the twentieth century it is unnecessary to believe in the supernatural any more.

The facts, however, point in exactly the opposite direction. The great world religions are thriving. Islam is spreading in Africa. Christianity is growing rapidly in parts of Africa too, as well as in South America and Asia. Even in Western Europe, where the number of people going to Christian churches every Sunday is falling, there is increased interest in alternative faiths such as spiritism, astrology and the Moonies. And the strength of religious faith in Eastern Europe — officially atheist countries — continues to puzzle the authorities.

Christianity and the supernatural

Christians believe in supernatural powers. Unlike some of the world's religions, Christianity teaches that God is person, not force. He is outside the dimensions of space and time, not just a force inside our minds.

The Bible says that there is only one God. This is a basic belief which Christianity shares with Judaism and Islam. But there are other spiritual beings too. Some are on God's side (his 'messengers',

Can the Christian faith survive in communist lands? The evidence shows it can and does.

● In the **USSR**, there are now twice as many Christians as atheists. More than one in three of all adults are church members. In the last ten years there has been a growth in the number of Soviet Christians, matched by a decline in the number of professing atheists.

● 25 years ago, when entry to **China** was difficult for westerners, a letter from a Christian reported: 'At first glance it would seem that the church in China has no hope. But in fact the opposite is the case. The church is daily growing stronger. At first, Soochow had only one place of worship but recently, because of the increase in the number of worshippers, it has been necessary to open a second place of worship.'

One way only

Unlike some religions (Hinduism for instance), Christianity makes exclusive claims. Jesus said: 'I am the way and the truth and the life. No one comes to the Father except through me.'

which is what 'angels' means). Others are not. Jesus himself believed and taught that the Devil is real and that demonic powers are active in the world.

This is why Christians are against all religious practices which dabble in the occult. Some of these things seem harmless enough, like playing with a ouija board or going to a seance. But a seance becomes much more than a game when powerful supernatural forces are at play. Those who contact spirits to use them or to gain power often finish up as their puppets. The Bible bans all attempts to contact the spirit world, apart from prayer to God himself.

The power of God

Christians believe that beyond human experience the universe is a battlefield for conflicting supernatural powers. But there is no doubt where victory lies. God remains in full control. The war is already won.

In this section of the book, the spotlight has fallen on what the Bible says about the creation and the very beginning of human history. It tells us that man and woman played into the hands of

evil by disobeying a clear command of God's. But God did not abandon them. He did not leave them to the fate they deserved. In promising the coming of Jesus, he promised that one day that defeat will be reversed.

When Jesus came, he showed God's victorious power in his miracles. As well as healing the sick, he got right through to the supernatural level — where human suffering has its roots — and expelled evil spirits from demon-possessed people. Those evil spirits always recognized his authority and obeyed his commands.

Then, at the end of Jesus' life, came the greatest miracle of all. He died and was buried. But then he came alive from the dead. By doing that he made it possible for his followers to have a new life as well.

A little while before he died, Jesus had promised them the power of the Holy Spirit to fight their battles. 'He lives with you', he told them, 'and will be in you.' After the resurrection when Jesus rose from the dead, that forecast came true. Later in the early Christian writings, Paul said 'I can do everything through him who gives me strength.' And it is the same today. Modern Christians do not follow a dead hero. They live in the supernatural strength of a living person.

Even in the twentieth century, the world's religions are alive and powerful. All good Muslims kneel to pray five times a day.

WHO WAS JESUS?

Myrtle Langley

2

It's a very special day — Christmas Day. All over the world Christians are celebrating the birth of Jesus Christ — which took place almost 2,000 years ago. They are celebrating a birth which changed history. For many people around the world, whether or not they are Christians, it is a public holiday, a time for giving and receiving presents, for enjoyment and rejoicing.

But that birth was not the end of the story — it was only the beginning.

Most people know something of the Christmas story — of a baby born in a stable, of angel songs, and the visits of shepherds and wise men. But is there something more to it than this?

Christmas is for the children – or is it? Does the birth of Jesus Christ have more to say to us than the tinsel and wrapping paper of the traditional Christmas?

Almost 2,000 years ago, a young woman called Mary lived in Nazareth in Galilee in the land of Palestine. She was engaged to be married to a man called Joseph.

'God saves'

Luke's Gospel tells us that before Mary got married the angel Gabriel appeared to her to tell her that she was going to have a baby. Mary was disturbed by this news. But the angel comforted her. It would happen, not in the usual way, but by God's will and by the power of the Holy Spirit. She would call her son 'Jesus', a Hebrew name meaning 'God saves' or 'Saviour', because this baby would 'save his people from their sins'.

For many years God's people had been looking forward to the coming of 'Messiah', God's 'chosen one', a 'king' who would save Israel. Now the time had come and Mary began to praise God her Saviour.

The birth of Jesus

Palestine was occupied territory — ruled by the Romans. Not long before Mary's baby was due to be born, Augustus, the Roman Emperor, ordered a census to be taken. Everyone had to go to his own city to be counted. Joseph belonged to Bethlehem, known as 'David's city' — Joseph was a descendant of the great king David. So Mary and Joseph travelled to Bethlehem.

Visitors

The noisy, crowded town wasn't the sort of place for a king to be born, but the Gospel accounts tell us that two sets of visitors came to see the baby. Shepherds, who had been told about this marvel by angels, came in from the fields where they had been minding their flocks to see 'the baby lying in a manger'. Wise men, who had studied the stars, travelled from the east to see 'the baby born to be king of the Jews.'

What does the word Christmas mean?

It means 'Christ's mass', from the Old English, Christ's feast day. Although we do not actually know the time of year Jesus was born, from the fourth century, Christians in Rome celebrated the birthday of Jesus on 25 December when the pagan world was having its mid-winter festival. This was held on 25 December or 6 January, according to the calendar used.

Santa Claus makes an unorthodox arrival on the island of Guadeloupe.

Find out ✱

Look at the beginning of Luke's Gospel.
Why did Luke write it?

Look it up

The angel appears to Mary Luke 1:26-28
The shepherds hear the news Luke 2:8-20
The visit of the wise men Matthew 2:1-12

The birth of Jesus

Only two of the four Gospels tell us about the birth of Jesus. Listed here are the events surrounding Jesus' birth.
● **Matthew, Chapters 1-2:**
The ancestors of Jesus
The birth of Jesus
Visitors from the East
The escape to Egypt
The killing of the children
The return from Egypt
● **Luke, Chapters 1-2:**
The birth of John the Baptist announced

The birth of Jesus announced
Mary visits Elizabeth
Mary's song of praise
The birth of John the Baptist
Zechariah's prophecy
The birth of Jesus
The shepherds and angels
Jesus named
Jesus presented in the temple
The return to Nazareth
● **Luke 3:23-38:**
The ancestors of Jesus

The future King

Many years before the birth of Jesus, the prophet Isaiah foretold the coming of a deliverer:
'A Child is born to us!
A Son is given to us!
And he will be our ruler.
He will be called, 'Wonderful Counsellor,' 'Mighty God', 'Eternal Father', 'Prince of Peace'.
Isaiah 9:6

A Christmas Prayer

A Christian's response to the birth of Jesus:
What can I give him,
Poor as I am?
If I were a shepherd
I would bring a lamb,
If I were a wise man
I would do my part, —
Yet what can I give him,
Give my heart.
Christina Rossetti
(1830-1894)

Why don't the Gospels tell us more about the life of Jesus?

Because the Gospels are neither autobiographies nor biographies. They do not tell us the detailed story of Jesus' life. There are no other types of book which are similar to the Gospels. Their aim is to show people the meaning of the life and death of Jesus.

Words

Priest: Simeon was probably a priest in the temple. The privilege of being a priest was passed down from father to son. A priest had the special task of representing the people to God.

Prophet: Anna was a prophet. There are many books by prophets in the Old Testament. A prophet is chosen by God to tell people what God is saying.

Covenant: This refers to the 'agreement' made between God and human beings. One modern example of a covenant is marriage. In the covenant made with Abraham, God promised to care for his 'chosen people'. Jesus came to make a new covenant between God and all people everywhere.

Find out ✿

● How did the three wise men know where to find Jesus? (Matthew 2)
● What is 'oral tradition'?

Look it up 🔍

Jesus is named Luke 2:21-38
Herod hears about Jesus Matthew 2:1-16
The boy Jesus in the temple Luke 2:41-52

The four Gospels do not tell us very much about Jesus from the time he was born until he was about thirty years old. But we do know that, like all Jewish boys, Jesus was circumcised and named when he was eight days old. Later he was taken to the temple in Jerusalem to be presented to the Lord — a custom for parents with every firstborn son. There, his parents offered a pair of doves or two young pigeons, as the law required.

God's promise

In the temple they met two old people — Simeon, the priest and Anna, the prophet. These were good, devout people who were waiting for God's promised Messiah. When they saw Jesus they started to praise God, for they recognized him to be Messiah, the 'deliverer', sent to bring God's 'salvation' and 'to set Jerusalem free'.

Escape to Egypt

But Herod the king felt threatened by a baby 'born to be king'. Hearing that he was likely to kill all the baby boys, Mary and Joseph fled with Jesus into Egypt. They returned after Herod's death.

The boy Jesus

Luke's Gospel tells us about Jesus as a boy. Every year, Mary and Joseph went up to Jerusalem for the Passover Festival, along with many other people. When Jesus was twelve years old he went too. He was now old enough to become 'a Son of the Law'. But on the way home his parents found he was missing. Going all the way back to Jerusalem, they found him in the temple sitting with the Jewish

Above A Jewish bar mitzvah in Jerusalem. A thirteen-year-old boy comes of age.

Left As a young boy, Jesus would have been taught by a 'Rabbi', or teacher.

teachers, listening to them and asking them questions. Everyone was amazed at his intelligent answers. When his parents expressed concern, he replied, 'Why did you have to look for me? Didn't you know that I had to be in my Father's house?' They didn't understand what he meant.

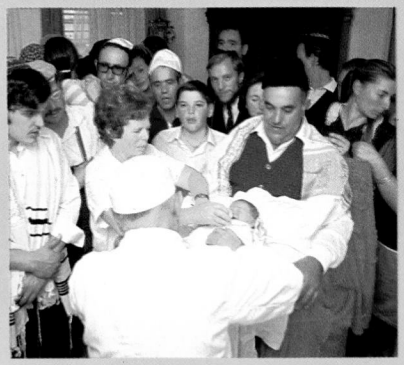

Why were Jewish boys circumcised?

Circumcision involves cutting off the foreskin of the penis. In Genesis we read about how God told Abraham, who started the Jewish nation, that Jewish boys should be circumcised at eight days old as a sign of his covenant with Israel, a sign that they were his 'chosen people', whom he had promised to love and care for.

2.3 WHAT DO WE KNOW ABOUT JESUS?

Archaeologists have unearthed documents, artefacts and even whole cities that tell us how people in the past lived. The ruins of Ephesus, in present-day Turkey, are an important archaeological site.

The key historical evidence for the life of Jesus is found in documents much older than any we have for the ancient classical authors such as Julius Caesar. These documents are the four Gospels: the accounts of the teaching, death and resurrection of Jesus by Matthew, Mark, Luke and John.

The rest of the New Testament (Acts, the Letters, the book of Revelation) has also been shown to be reliable. Scholars have checked out the details of the book of Acts, for instance: they agree with many discoveries made by archaeologists.

In these caves at Qumran by the Dead Sea, a collection of scrolls was discovered, dating from around the time of Jesus. The Dead Sea Scrolls have helped to verify the accuracy of the Bible.

People who knew Jesus

And then there is the Christian church — the followers of Jesus. Could the faith of so many millions of people rest on a person who was conjured up by someone's imagination? A man from a legend or myth? A fool or a madman? Could that sort of man inspire a faith so strong that for nearly two thousand years men and women have been willing to die for it?

Jewish and Roman Writers

Outside the New Testament there are a few significant historical references to Jesus:

● **Josephus,** the Jewish historian (about AD 37-100);
● **The Babylonian Talmud,** a collection of Jewish traditions passed on and then written down in the fifth century;
● **Pliny the Younger,** a Latin author (about AD 62-113);
● **Tacitus,** the Roman historian (about AD 55-117);
● **Suetonius,** the Roman writer (about AD 70-160).

Many scholars have puzzled over how the Gospels came to be written: what the sources were, whether one Gospel contradicts another in telling the same story, how we can understand the writer's meaning better.

Amazingly, the documents themselves have withstood the closest study that any documents in history have received! No major Christian belief is threatened by queries about whether bits of the story are authentic or not.

Christians met together on a certain day 'to sing a hymn to Christ as if to a god'.
Pliny the Younger

The Emperor Nero tried to put the blame for the great fire which destroyed half the city of Rome in AD 64 on the Christians. Tacitus, who describes Nero's persecution of the Christians in Rome says, 'Their name comes from Christus, who in the reign of Tiberius as emperor was condemned to death by the procurator Pontius Pilate.'
Tacitus

Words
Gospel — this really means 'good news'. The four Gospels — Matthew, Mark, Luke and John — were written to tell the good news about Jesus.

Find out
Throughout history there have been Christians willing to die for what they believe. Can you name any of them?

How did the Gospels come to be written?
Matthew, Mark, Luke and John, the four evangelists, used oral and written sources about Jesus to write their Gospels. These are dated somewhere between thirty-five and sixty years after the death of Jesus. Mark's is probably the earliest, and John's is probably the latest, but we don't know for sure.

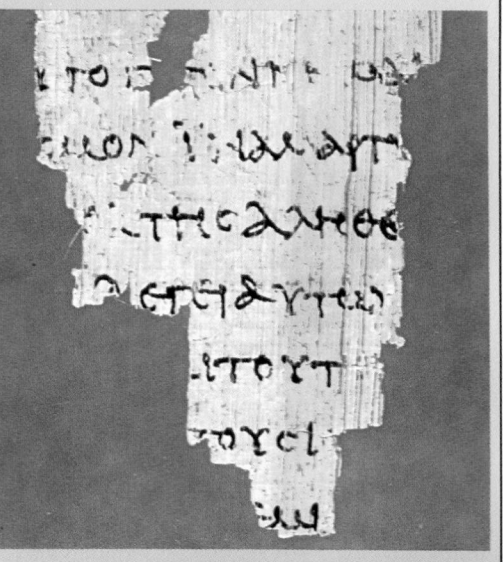

The oldest fragment of a New Testament book is this one from John's Gospel. Written in Greek, it dates from around AD 125.

For a fuller discussion of the Gospels and the other Bible documents, see Section 5, **God Speaks: The Bible.**

Jesus' life

Birth: shortly before the death of Herod the Great in 4 BC.
Baptism: at about the age of 30, probably in AD 27 or 28.
Beginning of public ministry: after his baptism.
Death: at Passover, probably AD 29 or 30.

The message of John the Baptist

'Turn away from your sins and be baptized, and God will forgive your sins.'

'John appeared in the desert, baptizing and preaching . . . He wore clothes made of camel's hair, with a leather belt round his waist and his food was locusts and wild honey. He announced to the people, "The man who will come after me is much greater than I am. I am not good enough even to bend down and untie his sandals. I baptize you with water, but he will baptize you with the Holy Spirit." '
Mark 1:4,6-8

Jesus did not begin his public ministry — 'the work God gave me to do' he called it — until after his baptism at about thirty years of age. As a young man he probably learnt the carpenter's or 'craftsman's' trade from his father Joseph in Nazareth.

John's baptism

The Jews were expecting a 'saviour', 'deliverer' or 'messiah' (meaning 'anointed one') who would save the country from foreign domination and at the same time crush their enemies. Many believed the Messiah would be a descendant of King David.

At the time Jesus was born, Israel was under Roman rule. So when John, a cousin of Jesus, began preaching in the desert,

many came to be 'baptized' — washed in the River Jordan or the pools nearby — thinking he was their Messiah.

John denied the claim. His baptism was of repentance for the forgiveness of sins. His message demanded that people change their ways, turn away from their selfish lives to prepare for one who was still to come, a man much greater than John himself.

The baptism of Jesus

Matthew tells us that when Jesus came to John to be baptized, John was amazed. He exclaimed, 'I ought to be baptized by you and yet you have come to me.'

But Jesus insisted that he too wanted to do what God required and so John agreed. As Jesus

Straight after his baptism, Jesus went out into the desert for forty days.

prayed after his baptism, the heavens opened and the Holy Spirit came down upon him in the form of a dove while a voice announced, 'You are my own dear Son, I am pleased with you.'

The testing of Jesus

Then Jesus was led by the Spirit into the desert where he was tempted by the Devil for forty days. The Devil tempted Jesus to get and use power in a wrong way — to turn stones into bread, to throw himself down from the highest point of the temple without getting hurt, and to accept all the kingdoms of the world and their wealth from the Devil.

Each time, Jesus replied, 'the scripture says . . .' Each time the Devil was defeated. Jesus knew that his power was going to come from serving God alone.

Does God — who is portrayed in the Bible as loving and kind — tempt us to do wrong?
No. God may test us, as a father tests his children or a carpenter tests a chair he has made. He is trying to find out if we can stand up to the test. It is Satan — the Devil — who tries to get us to do wrong.

Think about it . . .
If two trees are blown about in a great storm, the one which does not break bears the most strain.
  Think of the times when you have been tempted to do wrong. Which is easier — to give in or to resist? Which of the two helps to build up your character?

Words
Repentance — it really means 'change of mind' or 'change of heart' or to turn away from something. People who repent turn away from their past life to follow Jesus.
Baptism — Jesus commanded his followers to be baptized. In baptism the person is 'washed' or sprinkled with water as a sign of being made clean and starting a new life.

Look it up
Jesus is baptized Matthew 3:13-17
Jesus is tempted Matthew 4:1-11

2.5 GOOD NEWS OF THE KINGDOM

What did Jesus mean by the kingdom?

The Jews expected that Messiah would not only crush their enemies but also rule over them in everlasting peace and prosperity. This was a political hope. But Jesus announced the rule of God over *all* creation and over *all* people. Under God's rule, the whole creation will eventually be restored. In Jesus there began a new age, a fresh start. This was shown as Jesus confronted evil through his preaching, teaching and healing.

After his baptism Jesus spent the next two to three years travelling about the countryside preaching, teaching and healing. Much of that time was spent in Galilee but he travelled to Judea at least twice and perhaps even more frequently.

Forgiveness and new life

The first chapter of Mark's Gospel tells us what Jesus began to do in Galilee. He started announcing the good news.

'The right time has come,' he said, 'and the kingdom of God is near! Turn away from your sins and believe the good news!'

In the coming and preaching of Jesus, God's new rule had begun in the world. People could have their sins forgiven and receive new life. The start of this new life Jesus came to bring is seen in his actions: preaching and teaching, healing, miracles, casting out evil spirits.

Jesus once said, 'I have come to give you life in all its fullness.' To be a Christian means to hear and respond to the good news of Jesus.

Fishermen follow Jesus

As Jesus walked by the shore of Lake Galilee he saw two brothers, Simon and Andrew. They were catching fish with a net. Two other brothers, James and John, were getting their nets ready.

He called all four, saying, 'Come with me and I will teach you to catch men.' They became the first of Jesus' many disciples.

Jesus casts out an evil spirit

Mark tells us that as Jesus taught in the synagogue at Capernaum on the sabbath, a man with an evil spirit cried out. But Jesus ordered the spirit to be quiet and to come out of him. The people were amazed. Who was this man with power and authority to give orders to evil spirits and they obeyed him?

So the news about Jesus spread quickly throughout Galilee.

Jesus heals many people

Simon's mother-in-law was at home in bed sick with a fever when Jesus arrived with his disciples. He took her by the hand and helped her up. Soon she was well enough to wait on them at table.

Later, after the sun had set and evening had come, people came to Jesus. Mark tells us, 'All the people of the town gathered in front of the house.' And Jesus healed many people who were sick and drove out the demons. This was only the start of Jesus' ministry.

Words

Disciple — a follower of Jesus. The word really means a 'learner'. Jesus had many disciples — and the twelve disciples were chosen specially to be close friends.
Sabbath — the day of rest. For Jews this is a Saturday; for Christians it became Sunday because this was the day of the resurrection of Jesus.
Synagogue — the local Jewish meeting-place and (in Jesus' time) school. The main focus was the set of scrolls on which the Jewish law was written.

Jesus' first followers were ordinary working men. There are still fishermen on the Sea of Galilee.

Healing

'One Sunday, a few years ago, I enjoyed spending a Sunday with friends in a church in Kenya. The day began with a baptism by the riverside. Then there was a service of testimony, holy communion and preaching in the church building. At one point the pastor invited anyone who wished to be 'made whole' — to receive healing — to move forward to the altar rails to pray. A mother and her baby came forward. He laid hands on them, and prayed for God's blessing and the healing of body, mind and spirit, as God willed. I felt this showed that God's care for his people is constant and not only when they have a particular illness.'

Who were the poor?

In Palestine in the time of Jesus a minority led a life of luxury: the rulers and their court, the priestly aristocracy of Jerusalem, wealthy merchants, the chief tax collectors and the great landowners. The middle class was made up of craftsmen and country priests (the small farmers who were often in debt were closer to being peasants). The poorest people were the workers, the day-labourers, the slaves, the unemployed who resorted to begging and the disabled who relied on alms — money collected specially to help poor people.

The poor were those at the bottom of the heap who felt so helpless, powerless and oppressed that they looked to God alone for their deliverance. They believed that when Messiah came, he would proclaim 'God's year of Jubilee (favour)'. This was a time when debts would be cancelled, prisoners set free and land restored to its rightful owners.

Jesus in the synagogue at Nazareth

Jesus stood up to read from the prophet Isaiah.
'The Spirit of the Lord has been given
    to me,
for he has anointed me,
He has sent me to bring the good
    news to the poor,
to proclaim liberty to captives
and to the blind new sight,
to set the downtrodden free,
to proclaim the Lord's year of favour.'
Luke 4:18-19, quoting from Isaiah 61:1-2 and 58:6

The news about Jesus spread throughout the whole of Galilee. He taught in the synagogues and was praised by everyone.

Good news for the poor

One sabbath Jesus went as usual to the synagogue in Nazareth where he had been brought up. It was quite usual to ask any man who was educated to read from the Law and the Prophets in the Old Testament and to deliver a sermon.

Jesus chose a key passage from the prophet Isaiah. At the end of the reading Jesus told them how the prophecy had come true — that very day!

The people were impressed and astonished. God's kingdom, the time of the Messiah, had come, bringing healing, forgiveness and liberation . . .

Jesus is rejected

As they listened further they began to have doubts. Surely this man Jesus was only the son of Joseph? So Jesus reminded them that no prophet was ever welcome in his home town. Even the prophet Elijah was sent by God in a time of famine to a place outside Israel. The prophet Elisha was sent to heal Naaman the Syrian's skin-disease even though there were many who needed healing in Israel.

What Jesus meant was clear: this message of healing, forgiveness and liberation could be rejected by Israel — God's 'chosen people' — and offered to the Gentiles. In fact, Jesus had not finished the quotation from Isaiah. He had not mentioned the day of vengeance which Jews felt would fall on Gentiles, while they themselves would be saved.

So the people in the synagogue became very angry and dragged Jesus out of town to the top of a cliff to throw him down. But Jesus slipped through the crowd and walked away.

Who were the Gentiles?

The Gentiles were the nations other than God's 'chosen people' Israel. They were the non-Jews. Because they were God's 'chosen people', the Jews were supposed to show the Gentiles what God is like. This is a responsibility they often failed to take on. See the story of Jonah for instance — Jonah ran away from the idea of preaching to the great Gentile city of Nineveh.

A group of Christians meet to study the Bible.

Good news for the world

One of the themes in the Gospels is that Jesus came *first* to the people of Israel. But this does not mean that the good news is only for the Jewish people — it is for the whole world. Luke's Gospel makes a special point of this.

Think about it . . .

Why do you think the people in Nazareth, Jesus' home town, rejected him?

Check ✔

What was the sabbath? What was a synagogue?

Look it up 🔍

The events recorded in this chapter are from Luke, chapter 4.

2.7 JESUS THE TEACHER

Teaching in an African school. Jesus, too, was a teacher. But his classroom was wherever he could get a hearing, and his students were those who sometimes travelled miles to hear him.

Jesus says goodbye

In John's Gospel (chapters 14-17) Jesus tells his disciples that he will soon be leaving them. Yet they must not be upset because he is going ahead to prepare a place for them in heaven. In the meantime he will send them 'a Comforter', the Holy Spirit. The Spirit will come alongside them to strengthen and encourage them. He will make them continually aware of the presence of Jesus. He will also teach them and lead them to the truth. Then, at the end, Jesus himself will return and take them home to be with him for ever.

After the death of Jesus and at Pentecost (the coming of the Holy Spirit) Jesus' disciples remembered those words.

Jesus was a brilliant teacher. He was always watching what was going on round about him. So when he came to teach, he used real-life situations to bring his stories to life. People flocked round him. He always had something interesting and exciting to say.

The Sermon on the Mount

In his Sermon on the Mount Jesus delivered a new 'law'. It is a law of love. It does not contradict the Law of the Old Testament but develops the spirit underlying the Ten Commandments. Jesus' followers should:

● set their hearts first of all on God's kingdom and God's righteousness;
● love their enemies as well as their neighbours;
● be 'the salt of the earth' — no longer tasteless;
● be 'the light of the world' — no longer hidden.

It is what lies behind the Law that matters, Jesus said. For example: 'You have heard that people were told in the past, "Do not commit murder; anyone who does will be brought to trial." But now I tell you: whoever is angry with his brother will be brought to trial . . .'

The two builders

Jesus then told a story about two builders. The person who listens to Jesus' words and acts on them is like a wise man who builds his house on rock, but the person who listens and does not act on them is like a man who builds his house on sand. When the storms come on, one stands, the other falls.

For the small group of disciples, the teaching of Jesus was revolutionary. It turned accepted standards upside down. It is not the rich and famous who are happy; it is those who are pure in heart, the helpless, those who hunger and thirst for what is right . . .

True Happiness

Happy are the poor in spirit;
  theirs is the kingdom of heaven.
Happy are those who mourn;
  they shall be comforted.
Happy are those who are helpless;
  they shall have the earth for their heritage.
Happy are those who hunger and thirst for what is right;
  they shall be satisfied.
Happy are the merciful;
  they shall have mercy shown them.
Happy are the pure in heart;
  they shall see God.
Happy are the peacemakers;
  they shall be called children of God.
Happy are those who are persecuted in the cause of right;
  theirs is the kingdom of heaven.
Happy are you when people insult you and persecute you
  and speak all kinds of evil against you on my account.
Jesus, in Matthew 5:3-11

The Lord's Prayer

Jesus taught his disciples how to pray:

'Our Father in heaven:
May your holy name be
    honoured;
may your kingdom come;
may your will be done on earth as
    it is in heaven.
Give us today the food we need.
Forgive us the wrongs we have
    done, as we forgive the wrongs
    that others have done to us.
Do not bring us to hard testing but
    keep us safe from the Evil One.'
Jesus, in Matthew 6:9-13

Stories with a point

Jesus' most outstanding teaching is contained in his parables. These are lively stories, based on real-life situations. Jesus used them to put across a single point — something which invited a response.

God's kingdom is like . . .

Jesus used parables to tell a series of picture-stories about God's kingdom. Each story begins: 'God's kingdom is like . . .'

● A man takes the smallest of seeds, a mustard seed, and plants it in the ground. After a while it grows and becomes the biggest of all plants, putting out such large branches that the birds come and make nests in its shade.

● A woman takes yeast and mixes it with flour. Yeast spreads and makes the bread rise.

● Treasure is hidden in a field. Someone finds it and covers it up again quickly. He goes away happy, and sells everything he owns to buy the field.

● A merchant is looking for fine pearls. When he finds one of great value, he sells everything he owns and buys it.

● A dragnet is cast into the sea. When it is full, the fishermen haul it ashore. Then they collect the good fish in a basket and throw away those which are of no use. This is how it will be at the end of time when the evil people will be separated from the good people.

So, God's rule:

● grows from small beginnings;
● brings joy and is very valuable;
● will separate good from evil at the end of time.

Lost and found

God does not say, 'If you are good, then I will love you.' His love reaches out to sinners and outcasts. Jesus showed this in three parables — the lost sheep, the lost coin and the lost son (see Luke chapter 15). The message of the stories is that God seeks, finds and welcomes home those who are 'lost'. God's love is not earned — it is freely offered to all who want to receive it. This is important (and difficult) for people today who think that you have to be good to be a Christian or be accepted by God.

If God is our Father and he wants to show his love for us by giving us gifts, why do we need to pray?

Because, like our parents, God likes us to show our love and dependence on him by saying 'please' and 'thanks'.

Left *Jesus used ordinary, everyday events to teach people about God. In many respects, everyday life in the Middle East has changed little since Jesus' time. Here a Bedouin woman from Jordan makes unleavened bread.*

Think about it . . .
Look at each verse of True Happiness (sometimes called the Beatitudes). Are these things still important in our world today? Why?

Look it up

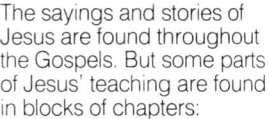

The sayings and stories of Jesus are found throughout the Gospels. But some parts of Jesus' teaching are found in blocks of chapters:
The Sermon on the Mount Matthew 5-7
The parables of the kingdom Matthew 13
Jesus predicts the end Luke 21
Jesus says goodbye to his disciples and prepares them for the future John 14-17

The lost sheep
The lost coin
The lost son
In Luke 15

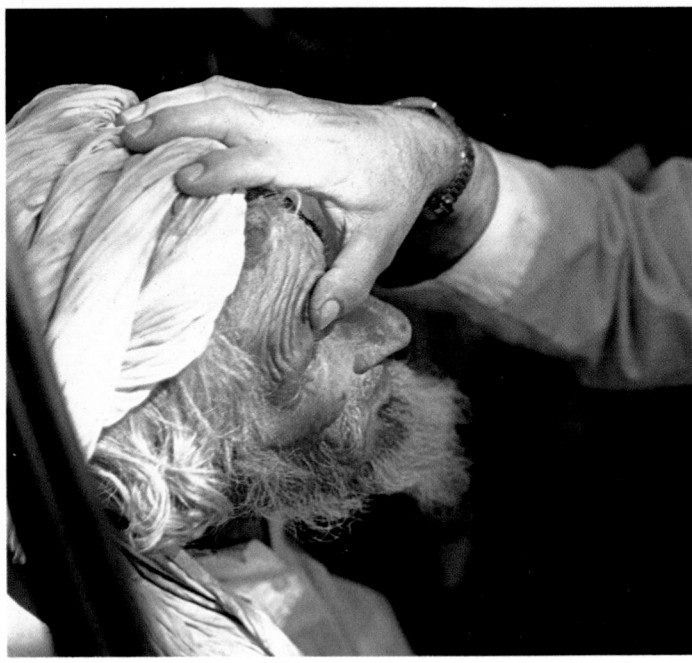

Jesus responded to human need by healing those who were ill. Modern Christians follow him in their medical work. Here a patient is examined at a roadside clinic in Pakistan.

When he healed people, Jesus showed his great love and compassion towards all who suffered. But he not only healed bodily diseases — he also forgave sins. The forgiveness of sins showed that Jesus came to bring healing for the whole person — healing of the body and of the mind and spirit.

In other words, when Jesus healed people and forgave their sins, it was a sign of complete healing, of wholeness. All need to be forgiven — some need to be made well too.

There are many accounts of Jesus healing people in the Gospels.

Jesus heals a paralyzed man

One day Jesus was in Capernaum. Immediately the word got round. So many people arrived at the house to see Jesus that there was no room, even around the front door.

While Jesus was teaching inside, four men carrying a friend on a mat arrived. Because they could not get in by the door, they took the paralyzed man up on to the roof, made a hole in it and let him down into the house!

When Jesus saw their faith he said to the man, 'My son, your sins are forgiven.' When some of the scribes objected to Jesus' forgiving sins, Jesus just told the man to pick up his mat and walk. This was as much as to ask 'What's the difference?'

Jesus heals a blind man

As Jesus was walking along with his disciples he saw a man who had been blind from birth. 'Teacher,' asked his disciples, 'whose sin caused him to be born blind, his own or his parents?'

'Neither,' replied Jesus, 'he was born blind so that God's power might be seen at work in him.' And with these words he spat on the ground, made a paste, spread it

Think about it . . .
Did Jesus classify people as 'good' and 'bad'?
What was his response to them? Why?

Look it up
Jesus heals a paralyzed man Mark 2:1-12
Jesus heals a blind man John 9:1-12

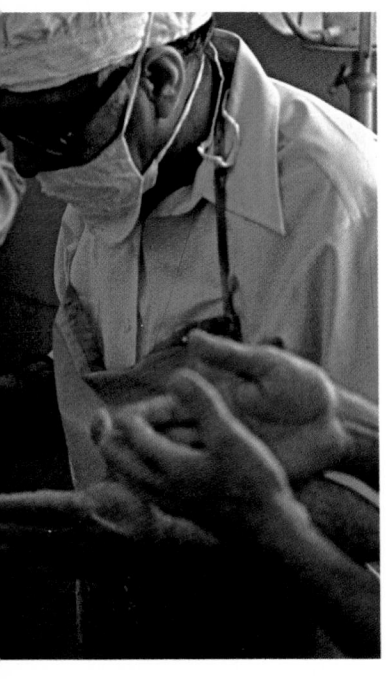

over the eyes of the blind man and said to him, 'Go and wash in the Pool of Siloam.' So the blind man went away, washed himself and came back seeing.

This caused an uproar among the people — and an investigation by the Pharisees, who held the view that illness must be caused by sin. They thought that 'bad' people deserved their suffering, while 'good' people (like themselves) deserved God's favour.

Jesus responded to this by saying, 'It is not those who are well who need a doctor, but those who are sick.'

Left *A Christian doctor in Pakistan prays with his patient before performing a cataract operation.*

Why did people flock to see Jesus?

In all the Gospel accounts Jesus showed great love and pity towards anybody in need. His love was acted out in making people 'whole' — healthy and renewed in body, mind and spirit. This wholeness was a sign that in Jesus God's kingdom had come.

Sin and suffering

In Bible times it was widely believed that there was a direct connection between sin and suffering, righteousness and success, long life, large families and being rich. Long life and riches were associated with God's favour; misfortune, disease and poverty were thought to be due to God's displeasure.

In the Old Testament the book of Job took up this theme — and said it wasn't true! Job's misfortunes and illness were not due to his behaviour — he was a good and righteous man. Job never knew the reason for his suffering — but he did learn something about the sovereign power and wisdom of God. Certainly sin in general has led to illness and suffering. But a person's illness or misfortune are not necessarily because of individual sin.

Human suffering is a fact that cannot be ignored. This German war cemetery from World War II contains 12,000 graves.

The Gospels tell us about many miracles which Jesus did. He appears to have had extraordinary power over nature, evil spirits and all kinds of diseases.

The words or phrases used to describe these supernatural acts, or miracles, are 'mighty works', 'wonders' and 'signs'.

● **Mighty works** emphasize the great power which Jesus had, which he said came from God his Father.

● **Wonders** show the wonder and amazement of the people who witnessed his miracles.

● **Signs** refer to the coming of God's kingdom which Jesus showed in his miracles. Satan, the enemy of God, is being challenged and put to flight. Such miraculous signs, as the Jewish people well knew, were only to be expected with the coming of God's kingdom. So what Jesus *did* backed up what he *said* about himself.

Calming the storm

Jesus showed his power over the forces of nature. He was crossing the Lake of Galilee in a boat with his disciples. Suddenly a strong wind blew up and the waves began to spill over into the boat, so that it was about to fill with water. A sudden storm like this was quite common.

The disciples were frightened,

Healing today

This is an account of healing in Indonesia today.

'Dr Sung encouraged the sick to realize that healing depended on the will of the Lord. He said, 'I cannot guarantee that all the sick among you will be healed. Even the Lord Jesus did not heal all then sick . . .'

After these introductory remarks the sick were then brought up to Dr Sung on the large platform one by one. As they knelt he anointed them each with oil in the name of the Lord and prayed with them.

That same afternoon a praise meeting was held in which those who had been healed gave their testimonies. Many had been cured of serious illnesses. A missionary wrote later, 'Blind people received their sight, the lame walked, the dumb spoke, the ears of the deaf were opened; and best of all, the cures have lasted.' So it was not just a case of auto-suggestion.
Kurt Koch

then annoyed as they saw Jesus sleeping with his head on a pillow at the back of the boat. 'Teacher, don't you care that we are about to die?' they cried out. Yet, when Jesus stood up and calmed the wind and the waves, and rebuked his disciples for their lack of faith, they were afraid, wondering what kind of man he was 'that even the wind and the waves obey him.'

Exorcising the spirits

On several occasions Jesus cast out evil spirits from people. So his power was over not only the forces of nature, but the forces of evil too. This was evidence of the final victory over evil that Jesus would

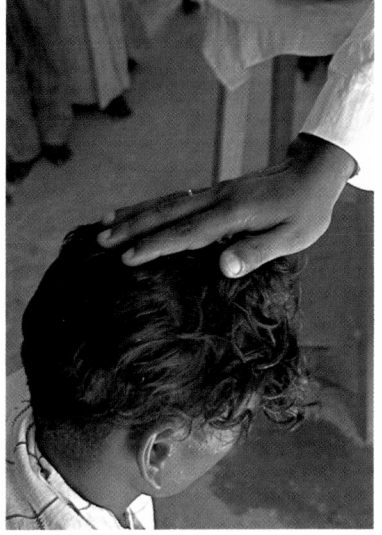

Jesus often healed people by touching them. On several occasions he touched lepers – an action that was both socially unacceptable and dangerous.

win on the cross, and evidence of God's rule.

Jesus even brought someone back to life. Lazarus had been buried for three days. Jesus was looking forward to the triumph of the resurrection, when he was raised from the dead. Jesus showed that he has power over life and death.

But even at the time of Jesus, like today, not everyone was healed. Jesus did not stop the whole process of illness and death — then. But it was to be only a matter of time! In the new age of his kingdom, suffering and death would be gone for ever.

So in the miracles of Jesus, and in Christian healing today, we catch a glimpse of the age to come.

How was Jesus different from other exorcists in his time?

Jesus cast out evil spirits by the word and power of God (the 'Spirit of God', the 'finger of God') as a sign of God's authority and rule over the powers of evil.

Despite our hopes and dreams, and our plans for the future, the only thing we can be completely certain about is that we will one day die. The Christian faith can help us to make sense of death, and to give us a hope that looks beyond it.

Look it up

Roman officer's servant
Luke 7:1-10
The man from Gadara
Mark 5:1-15
Calming the storm
Matthew 8:23-27
Walking on the water Mark 6:48-51

2.10 JESUS BRINGS CONFLICT!

Jesus was popular with the common people — for most of the time. But he was often out of favour with the power groups and special interest groups — the 'political' groups.

In Palestine there were many different groups — social, religious and political — which were not always on good terms either with one another or with the Romans, the occupying power. Jesus seems to have come into conflict with most of them — partly because they picked quarrels with him, but also because what Jesus did and said was controversial and revolutionary.

Picking a fight

From the beginning, the doctors of the Law, most of whom were Pharisees, found fault with Jesus.

Walking through some cornfields on the sabbath day with his disciples, Jesus did not stop them plucking ears of corn, rubbing them in their palms and eating them. The Pharisees objected to this — it was like threshing the grain and therefore not allowed on the sabbath!

Jesus replied that the sabbath was made for man's benefit and not man for the sabbath.

In the same way Jesus ignored objections to the healings he did on the sabbath. Surely it was better to do good rather than evil — even on the sabbath? This was only one of the many incidents recorded in the Gospels.

The Sadducees were even more hostile to Jesus than the scribes and Pharisees. They tried to trap Jesus in arguments about religious questions.

The followers of Herod Antipas — collaborators with the Roman rule — also tried to trap Jesus by asking him awkward questions.

The Pharisees, Sadducees and Herodians thought of themselves as important people — people with authority, especially about the Law

A man of authority

Jesus had an air of authority — no one who ever met him could deny it. All the arguments about the Law seem to start from this point. Where did Jesus' authority come from?

Think about it . . .
Read Mark 7:14-23. Do you agree with what Jesus says? Is it still true today?

Look it up
Jesus always had a ready answer to those who tried to trap him with trick questions — it wasn't always the answer they expected!
● **John 8:1-11** The Pharisees bring a woman who has committed adultery.
● **Matthew 22:15-22** The Pharisees ask Jesus about paying taxes.
● **Mark 12:18-27** The Sadducees ask Jesus about resurrection.

The religious groups

● **The Pharisees**
The Pharisees were the 'separated ones', who kept themselves apart from what was displeasing to God. They were usually good men, concerned for the holiness of God and the keeping of the Law. Through difficult times they had kept the true faith of Israel alive.

But their failing was 'legalism' — thinking that they could rely on keeping the Law to earn them a place in heaven. They had great zeal for keeping the Law in every little detail. But often it was just 'play-acting' — the original meaning of the word Jesus used of them — hypocrites.

● **The Sadducees**
The Sadducees were priestly aristocrats. They willingly collaborated with the Roman occupying forces for their own benefit. They were wealthy and worldly.

We are not certain of their beliefs. They appear to have accepted only the first five books of the Old Testament

(known as the Pentateuch, or the Torah) as authoritative rejecting the oral law of the scribes and doctors of the Law. They did not believe in the resurrection of the dead They behaved extremely harshly towards the common people and were among the greatest opponents of Jesus.

WANTED

THESE MEN ARE DANGEROUS

OSCAR ROMERO

Oscar Romero was a dangerous man. But he is no longer dangerous — because he is dead. He was a shy, quiet man, and the politicians of El Salvador who made him Archbishop thought they could easily manipulate him. They were wrong.

As Archbishop, Romero began to speak out in sermons and on the radio against violence, whether by government forces or left-wing groups. In March 1980 he was gunned down by four masked men as he celebrated mass. According to one report, his last words were: 'May Christ's sacrifice give us the courage to offer our own bodies for justice and peace.'

DIETRICH BONHOEFFER

When Adolf Hitler came to power in Germany in 1933, Dietrich Bonhoeffer, along with many other Christians, opposed him. He became active in the anti-Hitler resistance movement and spoke out against the inhuman Nazi policies.

In 1939 he refused a job offered to him in the United States — which would have given him a safe life. Instead he stayed in Germany, became a double-agent and was involved in a plot to assassinate Hitler. He was arrested in 1943 by the Gestapo for smuggling fourteen Jews out of the country to Switzerland.

He was hanged two years later, only weeks before the end of the war.

VALERI BARINOV

When Valeri Barinov wrote his rock opera, *Trumpet Call*, he did not realize what trouble it would cause him. For Barinov is a Christian and a Soviet citizen. At first, he was refused permission to perform the opera. When he appealed, his problems really started.

He was put under twenty-four-hour surveillance. Then he was arrested and committed to a psychiatric unit. His wife was told that his illness was 'abnormal beliefs'. He was injected daily with Larcactil — a powerful drug known to cause drowsiness and liver damage. There is no doubt that his arrest was directly connected with his Christian beliefs.

Valeri has now been sentenced to two and a half years in a labour camp.

DESMOND TUTU

Desmond Tutu is a Nobel Peace Prize winner and the Bishop of Johannesburg. But he is black. He is dangerous because he openly voices his opposition to the apartheid system of South Africa.

Why is the black majority in South Africa ruled by a minority of whites? Why are black people treated as an inferior race? Why are many men forced to live apart from their wives and children eleven months a year? And why are protesters imprisoned without trial?

Asking questions like these makes Desmond Tutu dangerous. People who say things like this have been arrested.

Jesus got into most trouble because he made friends with social outcasts — people whom nobody wanted. Respectable people were horrified to see Jesus and his disciples mixing with tax collectors and sinners, women and foreigners — considered to be the lowest people in society!

Tax collectors and sinners

Tax collectors were despised — they collected taxes for the Romans. They were also well known for taking more than their due — and pocketing the money.

One of the disciples was a tax collector before he left his job to follow Jesus. Zacchaeus, the little man who climbed up the sycamore tree to see Jesus, was a terrible cheat. But when Jesus invited himself to his home for a meal, Zacchaeus changed — he promised to repay people fourfold.

Samaritans and foreigners

There are stories in the Gospels which tell us that Jesus was ready to heal 'foreigners' as well as Jews.

Jews despised Samaritans: so when Jesus made a Samaritan the hero in one of his best known parables — 'The *Good* Samaritan' — people were scandalized.

Women

Jesus' attitude to women was revolutionary for a Jew and a teacher, a 'rabbi', of his time. Women were not regarded highly — they were definitely second-class citizens.

Jesus got on well with women. His relationship to them was easy and natural. He allowed women to touch him, accompany him, serve him and listen to his teaching.

Think about it . . .
- Is Jesus' attitude to women relevant to today's world?
- List reasons why you think Jesus said that a rich man would find it impossible to 'inherit the kingdom of God'. Might the same be true today?

Look it up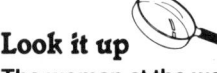

The woman at the well John 4:5-30
The woman with the haemorrhage Mark 5:25-34
The Gentile woman's daughter is healed Matthew 15:21-28
Jesus with Martha and Mary Luke 10:38-42
Jesus at the house of Simon the Pharisee Luke 7:36-50
The resurrection Luke 24:1-12

Jesus and women

In his time, Jesus' attitude to women was completely revolutionary:

- At a well in Samaria Jesus allowed a woman with a bad reputation (three times an outsider by virtue of being a Samaritan, a woman and a 'sinner'!) to give him a drink and talk to him in public. No wonder that both the woman

and the disciples were amazed and shocked.

● In a dense crowd he healed a woman with a haemorrhage who had touched him. By Jewish tradition she should not have touched him; and men would be considered ritually impure from her touch.

● In the border region of Tyre and Sidon — a 'foreign country' — he encouraged a Gentile woman to ask for her daughter's healing. He answered her plea with compassion and gentle humour.

● In the house of Mary and Martha at Bethany he praised Mary for sitting at his feet like a student at the feet of a teacher or rabbi. Jesus told her sister Martha off for being over-anxious about housework. Far from saying that a woman's place is in the home, Jesus' criticism was for a woman who was over-busy in the home.

● In Simon the Pharisee's house he allowed a sinful woman to wet his feet with her tears, wipe them with her hair and anoint them with precious ointment.

● At the resurrection he appeared first to the women and told them to announce the good news to his disciples.

2.12 FOLLOW ME!

Jesus' first words to his disciples were 'follow me!' The early Christians were known as 'followers of the Way'. Christians are people who walk in Jesus' footsteps.

The twelve disciples

'Jesus called his disciples to him and chose twelve of them to be apostles:
Simon (whom he named Peter)
and his brother Andrew;
James and John,
Philip and Bartholomew,
Matthew and Thomas,
James son of Alphaeus,
and Simon (who was called the Zealot),
Judas son of James,
and Judas Iscariot, who became the traitor.'
Luke 6:13-16

Jesus had many followers. There are three groups who are particularly mentioned in the Gospels:

● the women who were his friends, such as Mary and Martha of Bethany;

● the seventy disciples sent out on a special mission;

● the twelve 'disciples' or 'apostles' whom he chose to be very close to him. To these twelve he gave a special responsibility — telling people about him.

The disciples

The twelve disciples were a mixed bunch from varied backgrounds, different occupations, with different characteristics and personalities. The New Testament gives us vivid pictures of some of them, but we do not know very much about others. James, John, Simon and Andrew, were fishermen. They probably owned their own boats and had a flourishing business. Yet they left all that to follow Jesus.

● **James and John**, nicknamed by Jesus 'sons of thunder', are known for their stormy temperament and desire for power and greatness.

● **Andrew** is remembered for his interest in bringing others to Jesus.

● **Simon** (whom Jesus surnamed Peter, 'the rock') is the character who comes over most strongly in the New Testament. He is a man of action, the leader. He is impetuous, full of good intentions. He recognizes that Jesus is the Messiah. He swears everlasting loyalty — yet at the time of Jesus' trial, he denies even knowing him. Nevertheless, after the resurrection Jesus gives Peter the task of looking after his 'sheep' — the followers of Jesus.

● **Matthew**, also known as Levi, was a tax collector when Jesus

called him. He became, as far as we know, a loyal follower, and is named as author of the first Gospel.

● **Simon the Zealot** belonged to a nationalist group whose aim was to overthrow the Romans and free Israel.

● **Judas Iscariot** was the 'keeper of the purse', the group's treasurer — and the one who betrayed Jesus. Certainly in the Gospels he is portrayed as the kind of person who was ready to sell his Master for 'thirty pieces of silver'.

● **Philip** came from the same lakeside town of Bethsaida in Galilee as Simon Peter and Andrew. It was Philip who told Bartholomew that he had found the Messiah and who, with Andrew, brought the boy with five loaves and two fishes to Jesus.

● **Thomas** has been nicknamed 'doubting Thomas'. After Jesus' resurrection he was not present on one of the occasions when Jesus appeared to his followers. Thomas said he was unconvinced about the resurrection unless he could touch Jesus physically. When, eventually, he did see Jesus he simply exclaimed 'My Lord, and my God'.

● Of the remaining three disciples, **Bartholomew**, **James** the son of Alphaeus and **Judas** the son of James, we know nothing for certain.

Think about it . . .

What does Jesus' choice of special friends tell us about him?

Find out

Look up the following stories about Simon Peter.
What kind of man was he?
Matthew 4:18-19
Mark 8:27-30
Matthew 26:31-35
Matthew 26:69-75
John 21:1-19

PICTURING JESUS

Above Scenes from the life of Jesus are carved on this church door in Nigeria.

Above A nineteenth century depiction of Jesus that claims to be completely accurate.

Above Jesus has been pictured in many different ways down the ages. This medieval stained-glass view of Christ is in Canterbury Cathedral, England and dates from the thirteenth century.

Right Jesus as seen by a Chinese painter. This painting, on silk, shows Jesus teaching Mary Magdalene.

Above An African Jesus in Ethiopian stained-glass. Each culture sees Jesus as 'one of us', and not as a foreigner.

Left A Roman Catholic statue of Jesus from Peru.

Below 'The Light of the World' by the nineteenth century English artist Holman Hunt.

Below A Greek Orthodox icon showing the virgin Mary with the infant Jesus. It is not just a pretty picture. It is more like 'a window into and out of heaven'. Someone has said, 'You don't look at an icon. It looks at you.'

Left An eleventh century face of Christ from Alsace, France.

2.13 THE COST OF FOLLOWING JESUS

Christians meet to worship in Bucharest, Romania. This country is an atheistic state that actively opposes all Christian activity. The cost of following Jesus is extremely high for many people in today's world.

Think about it . . .
Make a list of reasons why someone might find it difficult to follow Jesus today.

Many people in Jesus' time, including the twelve disciples, went on believing that the Messiah's kingdom would be an earthly one, following an earthly pattern with rulers and ruled, high and low.

Called to serve

From the very beginning of his ministry — the time of testing in the desert — Jesus rejected the kind of power used by the political and religious leaders of his day.

His kingdom, his rule, would be different. Power and authority would be turned upside down. Instead of the leaders telling everyone else what to do, leadership would be by serving. The one who wants to be great must be the servant of the rest, and the one who wants to be first must be the last of all.

Called to carry the cross

Crucifixion, being nailed to a cross to die, was a cruel Roman method of execution. Criminals on their way to the place of crucifixion had to carry the cross-beam of their cross on their back.

Jesus used this picture when he warned his disciples of the cost of following him. Anyone wishing to follow Jesus must take up his cross daily — be prepared even to die for him.

'Whoever wants to save his own life will lose it; but whoever loses his life for me and for the gospel will save it,' Jesus said.

Called to sacrifice

The story of the rich young ruler shows us what Jesus asks of his followers.

This young man was happy to keep the commandments, yet he was concerned about eternal life. When Jesus challenged him and suggested that he sell all his possessions and give them to the poor, his face fell. And we read that he went away sad, because he was very rich.

Top A baptismal service held in secret in the countryside in the Soviet Union. These Christians can face severe penalties for practising their faith in this way.

So following Jesus has a cost. But, because God's values are not the same as the world's, no follower of Jesus ever finds the cost is too much.

One prayer puts it this way, 'To serve you is perfect freedom.'

Bottom A group of Christians meet to pray and read the Bible together in China. Despite official persecution for many years, the Chinese church is strong and growing. Restrictions have started to be lifted.

The Great Commandments

Jesus was probably the first to bring the commands to love God and neighbour together in the great commandments of love: '"Love the Lord your God with all your heart, with all your soul, and with all your mind." This is the greatest and most important commandment. The second most important commandment is like it: "Love your neighbour as you love yourself." '
Matthew 22:37-39

The New Commandment

'Jesus said to his disciples: "A new commandment I give to you, that you love one another as I have loved you. If you love one another, then everyone will know that you are my disciples." '
John 13:34-35

Sending Out the Seventy

Jesus also chose seventy disciples and sent them out two by two, to go ahead of him to every town and place where he himself was about to go. He said to them, 'There is a large harvest, but few workers to gather it in. Pray to the owner of the harvest that he will send out workers to gather in his harvest. Go! I am sending you like lambs among wolves. Don't take a purse or a beggar's bag or shoes; don't stop to greet anyone on the road. Whenever you go into a house, first say, "Peace be with this house." '
Luke 10:1-5

Look it up

Following Jesus Mark 8:34-36
The rich man Luke 18:18-30

2.14 JESUS FACES DEATH

Jesus predicts his death

'Jesus began to teach his disciples: "The Son of Man must suffer much and be rejected by the elders, the chief priests, and the teachers of the law. He will be put to death, but three days later he will rise to life.' He made this very clear to them.'
Mark 8:31-32

By now we can see that Jesus was not like the Messiah which most of the Jews expected. He did not want to be a political ruler, a king of the Jews to throw out the Romans and rule over an earthly kingdom. But this was not at all clear to the twelve disciples.

Peter's declaration

One day Jesus asked them who the people said he was.

They promptly replied, 'Some say that you are John the Baptist, others say that you are Elijah, while others say that you are one of the prophets.'

So then Jesus asked them, 'What about you? Who do you say I am?

And Peter immediately answered, 'You are the Messiah.'

But when Jesus began to prepare his disciples for his death it was Peter who took Jesus aside to rebuke him. Jesus knew that the elders, chief priests and doctors of the law would reject him, make him suffer and put him to death. Then, after three days, he would rise again. But Peter could not believe that this would happen.

Keep it a secret

In Mark's Gospel Jesus is portrayed as wanting his Messiahship kept secret. So Jesus tells his disciples not to let anyone know who he is, just as he had told the evil spirits, when they recognized him, not to tell others. Mark also tells us that the disciples did not really understand what Jesus was talking about.

The transfiguration

The transfiguration is the turning point in the Gospels' presentation of Jesus: Mark tells us that Jesus told Peter, James and John not to talk about it until after 'the Son of Man has risen from death'.

Jesus had taken the 'inner circle' of three up to a high mountain. Before them, he was changed into a shining figure, seen in conversation with Moses and Elijah, representing the Law and the Prophets of the Old Testament. Then a cloud appeared and covered them with its shadow, and a voice said from the cloud, 'This is my own dear Son — listen to him!'

The incident is usually seen as a foretaste of Jesus' glory after the resurrection.

But first he had to go to death — a horrible death, nailed to a cross.

Find out ✸

Read Mark 1:21-28,40-45; 5:1-20; 8:22-30; 9:30-32.

Why does it seem that Jesus did not want to let people think he was the Messiah?

The Jews rejected many of the prophets sent by God. Who were they? What happened to them?

Look it up

Peter's declaration
Matthew 16:13-20
The Transfiguration Mark 9:2-9

The death of Jesus was no accident. Jesus deliberately went up to Jerusalem, knowing that his enemies were plotting his arrest and death.

When Jesus spoke to the twelve disciples about the cost of following him and about the nearness of his death, they were all travelling together towards Jerusalem. John's Gospel actually tells us that Jesus set out for Jerusalem in order to die.

A prophecy comes true

In the Old Testament, Zechariah the prophet, in looking forward to the coming Messiah, had written:

'Tell the city of Zion,
   Look, your king is coming to you!
He is humble and rides on a donkey
   and on a colt, the foal of a
   donkey.'

Zechariah 9:9, quoted in Matthew 21:5

In this way Matthew explains why Jesus sent two of his disciples to a village near Jerusalem to get 'a donkey tied up with her colt beside her'. The prophecy is about to be fulfilled: Jesus is to enter Jerusalem as a humble king riding on a donkey! Can this be the Messiah the Jewish people have been waiting for?

Jesus loved Jerusalem

When Jesus was warned to leave Galilee because Herod wanted to kill him, he said, 'I must be on my way today, tomorrow, and the next day; it is not right for a prophet to be killed anywhere except in Jerusalem' and continued:

'Jerusalem, Jerusalem! You kill the prophets, you stone the messengers God has sent you! How many times have I wanted to put my arms round all your people, just as a hen gathers her chicks under her wings, but you would not let me! And so your Temple will be abandoned. I assure you that you will not see me until the time comes when you say, "God bless him who comes in the name of the Lord."'

Jesus, in Luke 13:34-35

THE EASTER FAITH

Myrtle Langley

It's Easter-time!
Millions of Christians
worldwide meet
together to remember
a vital fact of history.
Why?
And why is it that at
the heart of Christian
worship Sunday by
Sunday is an act in
which the church
shares together in the
taking of bread and
wine?

3

3.1 JESUS ENTERS JERUSALEM

Section 2, Who was Jesus? and Section 3, The Easter Faith look at what Christians believe about Jesus, drawing on the evidence in the four Gospels. Who was Jesus? followed the events of Jesus' life from his birth and childhood, looking at his teaching and the way of life he proclaimed. The Easter Faith takes up the story of the last week of Jesus' life — a week which changed history.

Jesus had talked about his death to his disciples. The Gospels tell us that Jesus knew he was going to die. It was no accident. But even as the time grew nearer, his disciples did not really understand.

The next few chapters tell the story of the first Easter — a dramatic, exciting story. The story is told from different angles in the four Gospels, but they all share in that same sense of victory which they saw in Jesus' death and resurrection.

We pick up the story at Jesus' entry into Jerusalem — riding on a donkey!

Jesus the King

When the two disciples brought the donkey to Jesus, they threw their cloaks on his back and Jesus got on. People crowded round. Some of them spread their cloaks on the road. Others cut palm branches from the trees to do the same.

As Jesus rode, the people shouted out: 'Praise God! God bless him who comes in the name of the Lord! God bless the coming kingdom of King David, our father! Praise God!'

In the temple

When he arrived in Jerusalem, Jesus went into the temple. In the Court of the Gentiles, he began to

The king on a donkey

Zechariah, the Old Testament prophet, foretold the arrival of the promised Messiah:
'Rejoice, rejoice, people of Zion!
Shout for joy, you people of Jerusalem!
Look, your King is coming to you!
He comes triumphant and victorious,
but humble and riding on a donkey —
on a colt, the foal of a donkey.'
Zechariah 9:9

drive out all those who were buying and selling. He overturned the tables of the money-changers and the stools of those who sold pigeons. These people were misusing the temple, cheating people and making money dishonestly.

The religious leaders heard about the incident — and from then on, we are told, they tried to find a way to kill Jesus. Yet they were afraid – afraid of the people and of public opinion. The people had been impressed by Jesus' teaching.

At Bethany

Matthew and Mark then tell us of an extraordinary incident in the house of 'Simon the leper' at Bethany.

A woman came in with an alabaster jar of very expensive perfume and poured it on Jesus' head.

Some of the people there protested strongly about the waste, but Jesus said, 'Leave her alone! Why are you bothering her? She has done a fine and beautiful thing for me . . . She did what she could; she poured perfume on my body to prepare it ahead of time for burial.'

Think about it . . .
Read the parable of the tenants in the vineyard in Luke 20:9-16.
Why do you think Jesus told this parable?

Jerusalem at sunset. The temple area, where Jesus drove out the dishonest merchants, is beyond the floodlit wall in the foreground.

Look it up
Jesus enters Jerusalem
Luke 19:28-40, Matthew 21:1-11
Jesus is anointed at Bethany Matthew 26:6-13, Mark 14:3-9

3.2 THE LAST SUPPER

It was just two days before the Festival of Passover and Unleavened Bread in Jerusalem. The city was crowded with people. The chief priests and the doctors of the Law were looking for a way to arrest Jesus. But they were afraid to risk it during the festival, in case the people rioted.

The plot

Judas Iscariot, one of the twelve disciples, gave the enemies of Jesus their chance.

We do not know why Judas

betrayed Jesus — perhaps it was because Jesus wasn't the kind of Messiah he expected.

Judas went to the chief priests who promised him money if he could find some way of handing Jesus over quietly.

The Passover

On the eve of the Passover, Jesus 'and his disciples met together in an upstairs room for the festival meal. John tells us that before they ate, Jesus insisted on washing his disciples' feet. This was the job of

A Jewish family share the Passover meal in their home. Hours before his death, Jesus celebrated the Passover with his twelve disciples.

...ervant or even a slave. Jesus washed his friends' feet to show that he had come to serve them by his death. It was a symbol of Jesus' love.

Then they ate the celebration meal of the Jews, commemorating the 'exodus' of the people of Israel from slavery — their 'salvation' many centuries before.

As they did so, they gave the traditional actions a new meaning. Jesus took a piece of bread, gave a prayer of thanks, broke it, and gave it to his disciples. 'Take it,' he said, 'this is my body.' Jesus' own

body was to be broken for them on the cross.

Then he took a cup of wine, again one of the traditional symbols of the meal, gave thanks to God, and handed it to them; and they all drank from it. Jesus was to pour out his own life-blood for them. As they shared the cup, so too they would be able to share in his death.

Jesus was to die for *their* sins, not his own — for the sins of the world.

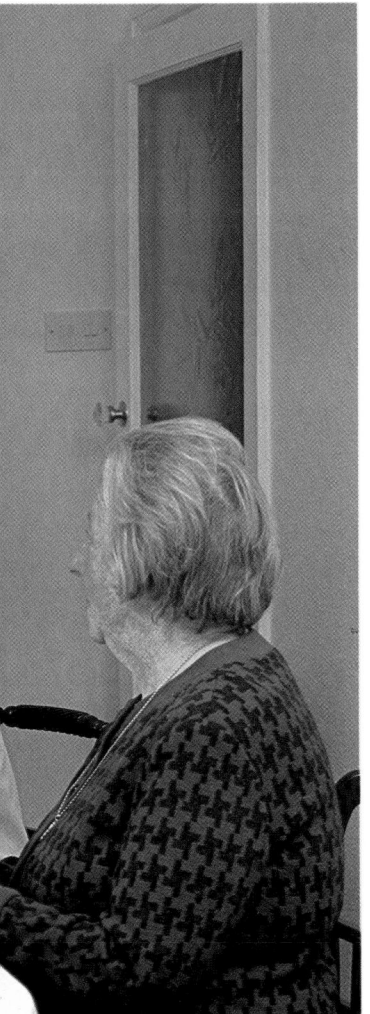

What was the Passover?

The festival of the Passover and Unleavened Bread was, and still is, one of the most important annual festivals of the Jewish people. It is a celebration of freedom and liberation, remembering how God delivered his people from slavery in Egypt. The angel of death 'passed over' the houses of the Israelites, whose doorposts had been smeared with the blood of lambs, but killed all the first-born children in Egypt. Read Exodus 12.

In Jesus' time thousands of pilgrims visited Jerusalem for the festival.

The Jewish Passover meal was to celebrate the liberation of the Israelites from Egypt. Christians see Jesus' last supper as a celebration of their liberation from sin and death.

Even Peter would deny him

After the meal, Jesus went with his disciples to the Mount of Olives. There Jesus told the Twelve that they would all run away and leave him. 'Not me', protested Peter, 'I will never leave you, even though all the rest do.'

It was then that Jesus warned Peter that he would be challenged that very night and that he would swear no less than three times that he never even knew Jesus. No one, not even his closest friend and follower, would be standing with Jesus when he took on the sins of the world.

Think about it . . .

Why did Jesus wash the disciples' feet?

Look it up
The last supper Matthew 26:26-30, Mark 14:22-26, Luke 22:14-20, John 13:1-30
Jesus washes the disciples' feet John 13:4-17

The words of Jesus at the Last Supper were recorded, not only in all four Gospels, but also, in their earliest form, by Paul when he wrote to the Christians in the city of Corinth:

'For I received from the Lord the teaching that I passed on to you: that the Lord Jesus, on the night he was betrayed, took a piece of bread, gave thanks to God, broke it, and said, "This is my body, which is for you. Do this in memory of me." In the same way, after the supper he took the cup and said, "This cup is God's new covenant, sealed with my blood. Whenever you drink it, do so in memory of me."'

Paul, in 1 Corinthians 11:23-25

All Christians use bread and wine to remember the death of Jesus. But they do this in many different ways. Here Baptists share the Lord's Supper in Korea.

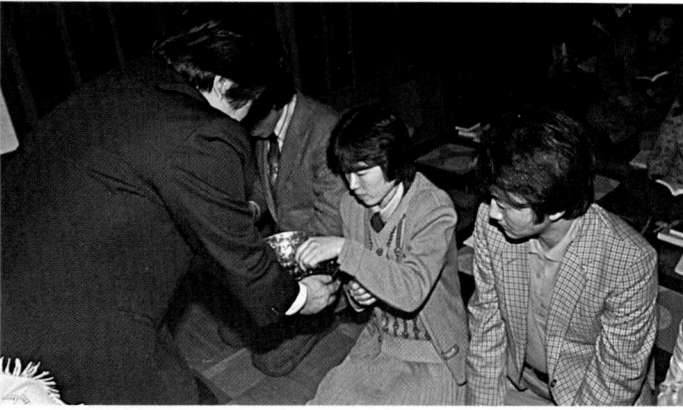

Why was this so important? What was it about the action that had to be underlined so heavily in the New Testament? And why do Christians today, all over the world, share bread and wine as Jesus asked?

Like visual aids, the bread and wine help Christians to picture the key events. But they are more than visual aids: they are a means of sharing in the events as well.

Just as the bread is broken, so Jesus' body was 'broken' on the cross. Just as the wine is poured out, Jesus' blood was 'poured out' in death. But why did Jesus die? He was crucified because of human sin, the evil that makes it impossible for people to share life with God.

Jesus was dying the death, the separation from God, which is the result of sin: he was dying *our* death!

Sharing

Just as Christians share the broken bread, going to a rail at the communion table or passing it from hand to hand, so they also share in the death of Jesus. If Jesus has died for them, they don't have to carry the burden of sinfulness and guilt themselves. They are forgiven. They can go free!

And that is not all. Jesus died. But as we shall see, Jesus also rose again from death. Christians can share too in the risen life of Jesus — new life!

***Left** An Anglican eucharist. One cup is used for the whole congregation to show that they are united by what Jesus did.*

***Right** Lutherans in South Africa celebrate holy communion.*

Above A priest of the Greek Orthodox Church administers holy communion.

Above The bread symbolizes the broken body of Jesus; the wine his spilt blood.

What names are used in your local church?

Different names used for the service today have different meanings or emphasize particular points in the service:
- **Eucharist:** From a Greek word meaning 'thanksgiving': the church meets to give thanks and praise to God for the death and rising again of Jesus.
- **Holy Communion:** The word 'communion' emphasizes sharing or fellowship: the sharing of people with God and with one another, as part of the church worldwide.
- **Mass:** Used in Catholic churches and others, the word comes from one of the final Latin words used in the service, 'missa': the people are sent out into the world. The mass is now usually in the local language, not Latin. It emphasizes the fact that the service brings the grace of God to the people; it is offered by the priest on behalf of the community as a re-presentation of the sacrifice of Jesus.
- **Lord's Supper:** This was a phrase coined by Paul the Apostle. The meal shared by Jesus with his disciples was a 'supper' — the Last Supper. Believers remember him in this way 'until he comes again' — until they share the celebration meal with him in the kingdom still to come.
- **Breaking of Bread:** The bread is broken and shared, the wine is also shared among the believers in a service which is usually simpler and less elaborate, emphasizing the 'remembrance' of the death and rising of Jesus.

Above A Free church breaking of bread service.

Left A Roman Catholic mass held in the open air in Brazil.

3.4 JESUS IN GETHSEMANE

Close to the Mount of Olives, across the Kidron Valley, was a garden called Gethsemane. It was an orchard of olive trees where Jesus and his disciples often went. After that last supper together, Jesus went there with his disciples.

Jesus prays

The Gospels show us that Jesus was always in touch with God, his Father, through prayer. In the garden Jesus took Peter, James and John with him to pray.

Jesus was vividly aware of his coming death. He turned to them and said, 'The sorrow in my heart is so great that it almost crushes me. Stay here and keep watch.' Then going a little further on he threw himself on the ground and prayed, 'Abba, Father, my Father! All things are possible for you. Take this cup of suffering away from me. Yet not what I want, but what you want.' He prayed this prayer three times, and three times he returned to find the three sleeping.

We cannot know what Jesus was thinking — but we know that it was not just fear of his physical death which made him pray in such agony.

Jesus is arrested

Then out of the darkness came men carrying torches. It was Judas, leading a crowd armed with swords and clubs, sent by the chief priests, the doctors of the Law and the elders. The signal was a kiss, and as soon as he arrived Judas went up to Jesus and kissed him — a kiss of betrayal. And so Jesus was arrested. He did not resist.

As Jesus was led away, all the disciples left him and ran away.

In the Garden of Gethsemane, Jesus struggled to come to terms with his coming crucifixion. It was here, too, that he was betrayed by Judas and arrested.

Think about it . . .
Why did the disciples run away?
What sort of people are they?

Look it up

Jesus prays in the garden of Gethsemane Matthew 26:36-46, Mark 14:32-42, Luke 22:39-46
Jesus is arrested Matthew 26:47-56, Mark 14:43-52, Luke 22:47-53, John 18:3-12

Jesus was totally human

The scene in Gethsemane is a striking example of Jesus' humanity. He drew back from death as any of us might. Mark's Gospel portrays Jesus as fully human. We are tempted — so too was Jesus; we grow exhausted and weary — so too did Jesus.

Mark portrays Jesus in his daily life: asleep on a cushion in the back of the boat; eating and drinking; experiencing joy and sorrow, laughter and anger. Yet the Bible stresses that Jesus was *fully* human — but without sin.

Unlike other Jews in his time Jesus addressed God as his father in the familiar language a child would use in talking to his 'daddy'. 'Abba' is the Aramaic, meaning 'Dear Father' or 'Dad'. He taught his followers to do the same.

3.5 JESUS ON TRIAL

Jesus faced a number of trials. One was held before Caiaphas, the High Priest, and the Council — the religious authorities. Another was before Pontius Pilate, the Roman Governor — the authority of Rome.

Jesus before the Council

The trial before the Council took place at night. There were no defence witnesses. It was a hurried affair — it was important to find Jesus guilty.

Jesus was accused by false witnesses. Their stories didn't even stand up to cross-questioning. Eventually Caiaphas, the High Priest, asked Jesus if he had any reply for his accusers.

Jesus remained silent.

So the High Priest asked Jesus if he was really the Messiah, the Son of God.

'I am,' answered Jesus, 'and you will all see the Son of Man sitting on the right of the Almighty and coming on the clouds of heaven.'

At that the High Priest tore his clothes, accusing Jesus of blasphemy, and asked the Council for its decision. They all declared him guilty and worthy of death.

Jesus before Pilate

But the Jewish leaders did not have the authority to put Jesus to death, so they handed Jesus over to Pilate, the Roman Governor. The charge had to be different. Pilate charged Jesus with claiming to be king of the Jews.

Jesus replied, 'So you say.'

Pilate tried again, but got no further. It was the custom at the time of the Passover Festival to release a prisoner — the one the crowd asked for. Pilate offered to release Jesus. But the people, encouraged by the chief priests, wanted him to release a criminal called Barabbas, and to put Jesus to death. 'Crucify him,' they yelled

So Pilate had Jesus whipped and handed him over to be crucified. And he washed his hands of the whole affair.

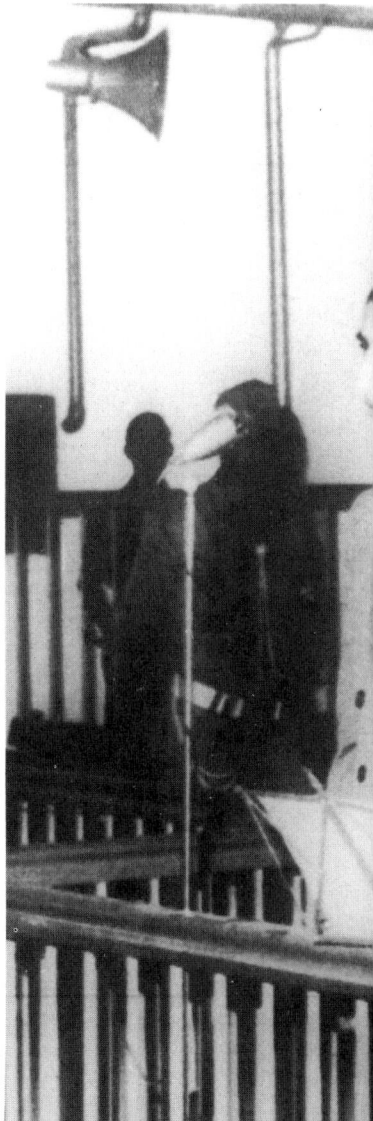

Jesus' trial was unjust — the witnesses could not agree with each other. But the verdict was guilty. Here a Turkish defendant is on trial for his life.

Think about it . . .

Read Matthew 26:69-75. Why do you think Peter denied he knew Jesus? What do you think Peter felt like when he heard the cock crow?

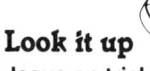

Look it up

Jesus on trial before the Council Matthew 26:57-67
Jesus on trial before Pilate John 18:28-19:16

Jesus before the Council

The Jewish religious leaders accused Jesus of blasphemy because he forgave sins (counting himself equal with God) and claimed to be Messiah. The penalty for blasphemy was death. But because of Roman rule, the Council did not possess the power of life and death.

Jesus before Pilate

The charges brought against Jesus before Pilate were that he was a political agitator, claimed to be 'king of the Jews', and so was a danger to political and social stability. Most scholars agree that the charge was unjustified, but that Pilate was a weak man who bowed to pressure from the Jewish establishment.

Pilate's wife

Matthew tells us: 'While Pilate was sitting in the judgement hall, his wife sent him a message: "Have nothing to do with that innocent man because in a dream last night I suffered much on account of him."' Matthew 27:19

Forgiveness

Read John 21. How do you know Jesus forgave Peter?

Quotations from the Old Testament on Jesus' death

'A hanged man is accursed by God' (Deuteronomy 21:23) was quoted by Paul as 'Cursed be every man who hangs on a tree' (Galatians 3:13) to support his view that Christ became a curse for us.

If Jesus was innocent, why didn't God step in?

God cared very much about Jesus' suffering. But Jesus came to offer himself up, an innocent person for the guilty. God does not always intervene in human affairs. He gives us freedom to exercise responsibility in our lives.

All Christians agree that the cross is central to Christianity — it is God's rescue mission to the world, and a symbol of his love for us.

But crucifixion was not a noble death — it was a horrible way to die, reserved for criminals. And Jesus had done nothing wrong.

The seven last sayings of Jesus

- 'Forgive them, Father! They don't know what they are doing' (Luke 23:34) — Jesus prays for those who were responsible for his death.
- 'I promise you that today you will be in Paradise with me' (Luke 23:43) — a promise given to one of the two criminals crucified with him who had said to Jesus, 'Remember me when you come in your kingly power' (Luke 23:42).
- 'He is your son . . . she is your mother' (John 19:26-27) — a word of loving concern spoken to Jesus' mother and to the 'beloved disciple' (usually thought to be John).
- 'My God, my God, why did you abandon me?' (Matthew 27:46; Mark 15:34) — an appalling and mysterious cry of desolate loneliness (quoting Psalm 22:1).
- 'I am thirsty' (John 19:28) — a pathetic cry of physical anguish and helplessness.
- 'It is finished' (John 19:30) — a word of accomplishment and victory.
- 'Father! In your hands I place my spirit!' (Luke 23:46) — a prayer of confidence and trust, cried in a loud voice as he died.

Mocked

Pilate handed Jesus over to the soldiers who took him to the courtyard in the governor's palace. They called the rest of the company together. They then stripped Jesus, clothed him in a purple robe, placed a crown of thorns on his head, and mocked him, saying, 'Hail, king of the Jews', spat on him, struck him on the head and knelt down in homage before him. When they had finished they took off the purple robe and put his own clothes back on him.

Crucified

As they led Jesus away to be crucified they met a man called Simon, from Cyrene in Africa, and made him carry the cross. When they arrived at the place of execution, Golgotha (the word means 'the place of a skull'), they offered Jesus wine mixed with a drug called myrrh, probably to dull his senses, but he refused to take it. Then they crucified him between two criminals. It was nine o'clock in the morning.

Afterwards, they threw dice for his clothes, while the passers-by hurled insults at him. At noon darkness came over the whole countryside and lasted for three hours. At three o'clock in the afternoon Jesus cried out with a loud cry, 'My God, my God, why did you abandon me?' and died. The curtain hanging in the temple was torn from top to bottom.

When he saw how Jesus died, an army officer, standing at the foot of the cross, said, 'This man was really the Son of God.' And the women from Galilee, and the other women who followed Jesus, looked on from a distance.

Buried

Towards evening, Joseph of Arimathea, a respected member of the Council who believed in the coming of God's kingdom, went to Pilate and asked for the body of Jesus. When he was sure Jesus was dead, Pilate gave his permission.

Then Joseph brought a linen sheet, took the body down, wrapped it and placed it in a new tomb.

It seemed the end of all their hopes. The promised kingdom was not to be. Jesus had died.

The events of the crucifixion

1 Pilate hands over Jesus.
2 Jesus is mocked by the soldiers.
3 Jesus carries his cross.
4 Jesus is offered and refuses wine spiced with bitter herbs.
5 The soldiers divide his garments between them.
6 Pilate writes the inscription 'The King of the Jews'.
7 Jesus is crucified with two criminals.
8 The passers-by and the religious leaders mock Jesus on the cross.
9 The criminals mock him.
10 Jesus dies.
11 An army officer cries out, 'This man was really the Son of God.'
12 His followers, particularly the women, look on from a distance.

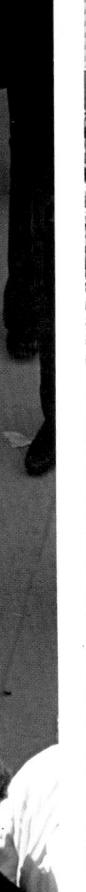

Far left *An Easter procession in Jerusalem follows the way said to have been taken by Jesus to his crucifixion.*

Left *A crowd of people played a large part in Jesus' death. They called for him to be crucified.*

Think about it . . .

Why do you think the army officer standing by the cross said, 'This man was really the Son of God'?

Look it up

Jesus is crucified Matthew 27:27-56, Mark 15:16-41, Luke 23:26-49, John 19:16-30

3.7 THE FIRST EASTER

We are not sure what exactly happened on the first Easter Sunday morning. But from the varied accounts in the Gospels we get a good general picture. Just as evidence given by eye-witnesses at an accident varies (although they all saw the *same thing* happen), so there are various accounts of what happened that first Easter morning.

The Easter story

Very early on the first day of the week some of the women, including Mary Magdalene and perhaps Mary the mother of James, and Salome, prepared spices to anoint Jesus' body. But when they arrived at the tomb it was open. They could not find the body!

They were given a message by an angel — and they were to go to tell the disciples. The women did as they were told, but the disciples wouldn't believe them, calling their story 'nonsense'. Instead, they went to see for themselves.

It was true!
Jesus had risen from the dead!

The facts

Two facts remain indisputable to
Christian and non-Christian alike:
● The tomb was empty. The
graveclothes had not been
disturbed — they had simply
collapsed and the body had gone
. . . from inside.
● The followers of Jesus, who had
deserted him at his death, became
totally convinced after that first
Easter morning that Jesus was alive
again. They had been miserable,
disillusioned. But they became
filled with a new confidence,
prepared even to die for what they
believed to be true.

They saw Jesus

We read in the four Gospels of a
whole series of appearances of
Jesus in the following days.

In **Matthew** Jesus appeared to
the women as they left the tomb in
a hurry to tell the disciples. Then he
appeared to the disciples themselves
on a hill in Galilee.

In **Mark** Jesus appeared first to
Mary Magdalene, then to two of
the disciples on their way to the
city, and finally, to the eleven.

In **Luke** Jesus appeared to two
of the disciples on their way to a
village called Emmaus, then to
Simon, and finally, to all the
disciples. On the first and last of
these occasions he ate a meal with
them (he wasn't just a ghost!).

In **John** Jesus appeared first to
Mary Magdalene, to ten of the
disciples gathered behind locked
doors for fear of the Jewish
authorities, then again when
Thomas was present, and finally,
to some of the disciples along the
shores of Lake Galilee, where he
had prepared for them a breakfast
of bread and fish.

If a lawyer was to weigh up
the evidence for the
resurrection, he or she
would look for two things:
● **Reliable witnesses:**
Paul, in his first letter to the
Corinthians, gives us the
earliest account (about AD
55). He must have obtained
this evidence from witnesses
within a few years of the
crucifixion.

Paul's evidence is
confirmed by the Gospel
writers. There are differences
in detail — but these tend to
strengthen the value of the
witnesses' testimonies.
● **Circumstantial
evidence:** *The tomb was
empty.* This cannot be
explained away by alleging
that the disciples stole the
body, the authorities
removed it, the women went
to the wrong tomb, or that
Jesus was not really dead,
only unconscious. If any of
the first three had been true
the preaching of the
resurrection could not have
continued in Jerusalem. The
authorities could simply have
produced the body. The
fourth does not stand up to
examination.

*The followers of Jesus
were completely changed.*
After his death Jesus was
seen for forty days. But long
after his ascension to heaven
he was seen by others, for
example, Paul on the road to
the town of Damascus and
John on the Greek island of
Patmos. Countless others
through the centuries have
believed he is alive.

Look it up

The first Easter morning
Matthew 28:1-10, Mark
16:1-10, Luke 24:1-12, John
20:1-10
**Paul testifies to the
resurrection** 1 Corinthians
15:3-7

The Gospels and the book of Acts tell us that Jesus appeared to his followers for forty days after his death. He appeared as a *real* person with a real body. He was not a ghost, neither was he exactly as he was before his death. We are told that he suddenly appeared in a room with locked doors. He ate ordinary food and drink. And he was seen on at least one occasion by more than five hundred people at once.

The Ascension

'Then he led them out of the city as far as Bethany, where he raised his hands and blessed them. As he was blessing them, he departed from them and was taken up into heaven. They worshipped him and went back into Jerusalem, filled with great joy, and spent all their time in the Temple giving thanks to God.'
Luke 24:50-53

Jesus' last words to his disciples

'I have been given all authority in heaven and on earth. Go, then, to all peoples everywhere and make them my disciples: baptize them in the name of the Father, the Son, and the Holy Spirit, and teach them to obey everything I have commanded you. And I will be with you always, to the end of the age.'
Matthew 28:18-20

Go!

During that time Jesus taught his disciples about himself and his mission. Then he told them to go out into the world and tell other people the 'good news' — the message of forgiveness and new life, of peace between people and God and with one another. His disciples must baptize any person who believed in him, and teach his followers the way of life of the new kingdom.

Stay!

But Jesus knew that his disciples were weak and frightened people. When he was arrested and crucified they had run away. After he rose from the dead they had listened with bewilderment and amazement as he explained how the writings of the prophets in the Old Testament had come true. Now he reassured them. He told them to wait in Jerusalem until the Holy Spirit, which he had promised to them, came to give them strength and power.

After forty days Jesus was taken up into heaven.

Look it up

Jesus appears after the resurrection Matthew 28:16-20, Mark 16:14-18, Luke 24:36-49, John 20:19-23, Acts 1:6-8
The Ascension Mark 16:19-20, Luke 24:50-53, Acts 1:9-11

How would you feel . . . ?

How would you have felt had you been the disciples, and why? Sad? Frightened? Let down? Puzzled? Fed up? Cheated? Hopeful? Angry?

The temple area is a holy site for the Jewish people. In the time of Jesus, Herod's Temple stood here and the Temple of Solomon had been built on the same site 900 years earlier. It was the focus of worship for the nation.

Jerusalem: Focus of Three Faiths

The Dome of the Rock, built on the temple mount, is revered by Muslims as the place where Abraham was willing to sacrifice his son, Isaac — but was stopped from doing so by God. The mosque is built around a great outcrop of rock.

The Church of the Holy Sepulchre is important to Christians as the probable site for the resurrection of Jesus from death. His tomb was found to be empty and he appeared to his disciples.

After Jesus was taken up to heaven his disciples went back to Jerusalem. There they chose a replacement for Judas. And they met together with the women, Mary the mother of Jesus and his brothers to pray.

The coming of the Spirit

The second chapter of Acts gives a vivid picture of the coming of the Holy Spirit:

'When the day of Pentecost came, all the believers were gathered together in one place. Suddenly there was a noise from the sky which sounded like a strong wind blowing, and it filled the whole house where they were sitting. Then they saw what looked like tongues of fire which spread out and touched each person there. They were all filled with the Holy Spirit and began to talk in other languages, as the Spirit enabled them to speak.'
Acts 2:1-4

Jews from all parts of the world were in Jerusalem at the time. When they heard the racket they went to see for themselves. To their amazement each of them heard the believers speaking in his own

On the day of Pentecost, Jesus' followers were filled with his Spirit. They received new strength and faith in believing in Jesus. Their joy and excitement made some onlookers think that they were drunk!

language about the great things God had done. They were excited and impressed and kept asking each other what it all meant. But there were others who made fun of them: 'These people are drunk!' they said.

The fulfilment of prophecy

Next, something incredible happened. Simon Peter, who had denied he knew Jesus and had run away, stood up with the other eleven disciples, now called apostles, and began to address the crowd in a loud voice.

'These people are not drunk, as you suppose; after all, it is only nine o'clock in the morning! Instead, this is what the prophet Joel spoke about.'

Then, quoting from the prophet's book in the Old Testament, he recalled that in the last days God would pour out his spirit on everyone. Sons and daughters, men and women, old and young alike would have dreams and see visions and proclaim God's message. And everyone who called out to the Lord for help would be saved.

Who is the Spirit of God?

● **At creation** 'the Spirit of God was moving over the water.'
Genesis 1:2
● **The prophet Joel:**
'Afterwards I will pour out my spirit on
    everyone:
your sons and daughters will proclaim
    my message;
your old men will have dreams,
and your young men will see visions.
At that time I will pour out my spirit
    even on servants, both men and
    women.'
Joel 2:28-29
● **In John's Gospel**, Jesus tells Nicodemus (the Jewish leader who came to him secretly by night): 'A person is born physically of human parents, but he is born spiritually of the Spirit.'
John 3:6
● **Jesus said** to his disciples: 'When the Spirit comes, who reveals the truth about God, he will lead you into all the truth.'
John 16:13
● **The apostle Paul said:**
'Those who are led by God's Spirit are God's children . . . and by the Spirit's power . . . cry out to God, 'Abba! my Father!'
Romans 8:15

Think about it . . .
'What happened on the Day of Pentecost is the strongest possible evidence for the resurrection.'
Do you agree?

A changed Peter, no longer weak and fearful but strong and bold, continued with his sermon which turned out to be a new message about Jesus.

Jesus is the promised Messiah

His message was that Jesus of Nazareth was a man whose authority from God was clearly proved to the people by all the miracles and wonders which God did through him. But God had let the people kill him. But then God raised him from death, setting him free from its power. The man whom they crucified, God made Lord and Messiah.

When the people heard Peter's words, many were upset. This went against all they had always been taught about the Messiah! But Peter continued, 'Each one of you must turn away from his sins and be baptized in the name of Jesus Christ, so that your sins will be forgiven; and you will receive God's gift, the Holy Spirit. For God's promise was made to you and your children, and to all who are far away — all whom the Lord our God calls to himself.'

The message of the first Christians

● The events which the prophets of old predicted have come to pass, and the new era has begun with the coming of Christ.
● He was born into the family of David.
● He died as the Scriptures foretold, to save us from the present evil times, and was buried.
● On the third day he rose again from the dead, as the Scriptures foretold.
● He is now at God's right hand in heaven, Son of God and Lord of the living and the dead.
● One day he will come to earth again as judge and saviour.
Summarized from the Acts of the Apostles.

Peter's audience on the Day of Pentecost
Believers scattered after Stephen's death
Paul spreads the good news

In the Book of Acts, the Holy Spirit was seen in tongues of fire resting on the head of each Christian. The day of Pentecost has been called 'the church's birthday'.

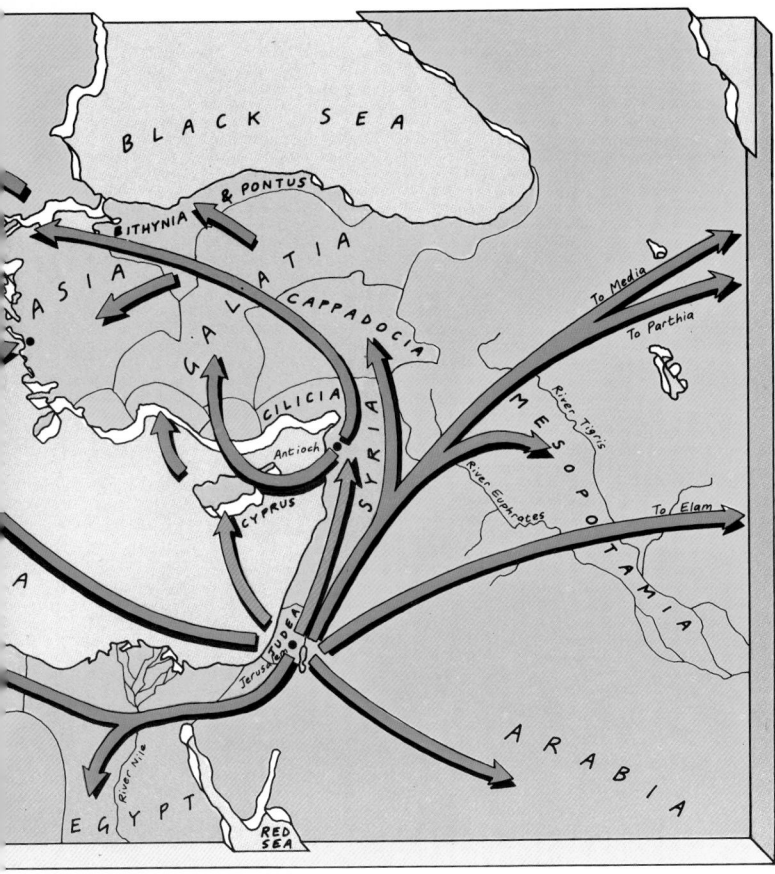

Find out

Ask someone who is a Christian what it was like when he or she heard the message about Jesus. What difference did it make?

The conversion of Paul

Saul of Tarsus was a prominent Jew. He hated Christians and he persecuted them.

Then one day on the road to Damascus, a bright light flashed around him and he heard a voice saying to him, 'Saul, Saul! why do you persecute me?'

'Who are you, Lord?' he asked.

'I am Jesus whom you persecute,' the voice answered and directed Paul to get up and go into the city.

Paul was so changed afterwards that he travelled throughout the Mediterranean countries, telling people about Jesus — people who were not Jews, but 'Gentiles'. So he was called the 'Apostle of the Gentiles'. He wrote many letters to Christians — which we now have in the New Testament. We know that he preached in Rome itself and that he aimed to travel as far westwards as Spain.
(Read Acts 9 for the story of his conversion.)

New people with a new message

About three thousand people believed the message and were baptized. The change which came over Peter and the rest of the disciples was amazing. It is this change as much as anything else which makes Christians so sure that the events of Easter, Ascension and Pentecost were essentially to do with new life.

The apostles had become new people with a new message. Jesus is alive and changes people's lives, bringing hope instead of despair, joy, instead of sorrow and replacing cowardice with boldness.

3.11 A NEW COMMUNITY

Christians have always had a strong sense of community. The first believers shared their money and possessions. Later, Christians lived and worked together in monasteries and convents. The L'Arche community in France is made up of handicapped people who share their lives together.

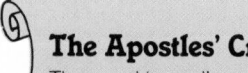

The Apostles' Creed

The word 'creed' means 'I believe'. One creed, said by many Christians, is called the Apostles' Creed. Despite its name it wasn't written by the apostles, but it sums up the basic beliefs of Christianity. It is one of the oldest creeds.
'I believe in God, the Father almighty,
creator of heaven and earth;
and in Jesus Christ, his only Son, our Lord.
He was conceived by the Holy Spirit,
born from Mary the virgin,
suffered under Pontius Pilate,
was crucified, died, was buried and descended to the underworld.
On the third day he rose again from the dead,
ascended to heaven and sits on the right hand of God the Father almighty.
From there he will come to judge the living and the dead.
I believe in the Holy Spirit,
the holy catholic church,
the communion of saints,
the forgiveness of sins,
the resurrection of the body and eternal life.

It wasn't long before the new people with a new message became a new community.

Belonging

This 'family' — the gathering or assembly of people — came to be known as the church. The church was open to all — Jews and Gentiles, slaves and free people, men and women — all who believed in Jesus and found new life in him.

Their new life, membership of the church, was expressed in baptism. All the old barriers of race, class and sex were broken down, all were united and equal in Jesus Christ. What a great joy baptism must have been for that first Christian community!

Above In any Christian community, worship is at the centre.

Bottom left Christians believe they are called to be servants of one another. In a community this means sharing in the cleaning and washing up.

Baptism

Baptism means 'washing': to be sprinkled with water or go right under the water in a baptismal pool or a lake or river.

In doing so, believers show that they share in the death and new life of Jesus. Their old sinful selves have been drowned! Jesus has died for their sins and risen again to bring new life. They promise to repent, to turn from their sins and live according to the teaching of Jesus.

When children are baptized, these promises are made on their behalf by parents or godparents. The promises are then 'confirmed' when the child grows up and accepts the faith personally.

So baptism or confirmation also marks the time when people are received into membership of the church. Just as they identify themselves with Jesus in his death and rising again in their baptism, so they can continue to do so in sharing the bread and wine of communion.

Sharing

The new believers who were baptized met together as a group day by day in the temple and for meals and prayers in their homes. Every day, there were new members. Then they began to share their belongings — selling their property and possessions and sharing their money.

Giving

Spending time together, praying and meeting for meals was important to the new community. But also of importance was looking after the poor, the widows and the sick, and spreading the good news of the gospel far and wide.

Although many people thought this new community was a branch of Judaism, the new message was bound to arouse some hostility from Romans and Greeks on the one hand and Jews on the other. It meant that Peter and John were put in prison, Stephen was stoned to death, and many believers were persecuted. The message spread out from Jerusalem into Samaria, Syria, Asia Minor (modern-day Turkey) and Greece, until it finally reached Rome itself, capital of the empire. The believers were first called Christians in Syrian Antioch (see Acts chapter 11, verse 26).

It is traditionally believed that the apostles Peter and Paul both died in Rome in the persecutions under Nero, the emperor who blamed the burning of Rome on Christians.

Find out

Try to find a local group of Christians who share their belongings and live as a community.

The Gospels are not biographies of Jesus. They have a very special purpose — they are a 'witness' to Jesus' life: they give evidence about him, and they were written to show us the meaning of his life, death and resurrection.

Jesus is given certain names and titles in the Gospels. Some names and titles were used by Jesus himself; others were given him by the early church as a way of expressing what they understood about Jesus — their Lord, who had risen, ascended and was now glorified in heaven.

Messiah or Christ

We know for certain that the early Christians believed Jesus to be the promised Messiah (*Masiah* in Hebrew; *Christos* in Greek), 'the anointed one', successor to King David. But they also saw him as 'a suffering servant' of all nations, rather than as a political ruler over the nation of Israel.

Lord

Many ancient gods were called 'lord'. In the Old Testament, God was called 'Yahweh', or 'Lord', but so too were the Canaanite gods or 'baals'. The Romans and Greeks called their gods lords. Roman masters were lords over their slaves and in everyday life 'lord' was a title of respect, like the English 'sir'.

But for the early Christians the 'lordship' of Jesus signified his rule over the whole universe, which would one day be recognized by all people everywhere. Paul in his letters uses the title no less than 222 times!

Son of man

In Hebrew there are no adjectives.

If you want to say 'human', you would have to say 'son of man'. 'Divine' would be 'son of God'. Jesus gave two of his disciples the nickname, 'sons of thunder'. It's not hard to imagine what their tempers were like!

Jesus often used the phrase 'Son of Man' to refer to himself as 'the fully human one'. But there was a twist to it: in the Old Testament the Messiah would be the 'Son of Man' coming in clouds of glory.

Son of God

The early Christians used the title to refer to Jesus' unique relationship to God his Father. At Jesus' baptism, his testing in the desert, his trial and his death, this title stands out. In the Son the Father is seen: 'Whoever has seen me has seen the Father.' If we have seen Jesus, we have seen God himself in human form.

I am

In the Old Testament book of Exodus we read how God revealed his personal name to Moses at the burning bush as 'I am who I am.' The Hebrew is 'Yahweh' and may mean literally 'I will be who I will be' or simply 'I am'. The name conveys the idea of a living, active and trustworthy personal Being.

In the New Testament, John's Gospel records Jesus' seven great 'I am' statements based on his saying, 'Before Abraham was born, I am':
- 'I am the bread of life.'
- 'I am the light of the world.'
- 'I am the gate for the sheep.'
- 'I am the good shepherd.'
- 'I am the resurrection and the life.'
- 'I am the way, the truth and the life.'
- 'I am the real vine.'

The first Christians had a number of symbols to express their faith in Jesus.

ΑΩ

- The **Alpha** and the **Omega** were the first and last letters of the Greek alphabet, meaning that Jesus is the beginning and the end of all things (Revelation 1:8; 22:13).

IC

- The initials of **Jesus** and **Christ** in Latin.

- The **Chi-Rho** sign was made up of the first two letters of the Greek word for Christ, *Christos*.

- **Ichthus** in Greek means 'fish'. It was used among early Christians as an anagram of the first letters of a kind of creed, meaning 'Jesus Christ, God's Son and Saviour.'

The lamb

The title 'lamb' is not used much in the New Testament, but it did become a common way of understanding who Jesus was in the early church.

Above anything else, the lamb was the animal of Jewish sacrifice, especially at Passover, when it was recalled that the blood of a young, pure, male lamb was sprinkled on the doorposts and saved Israel from death in Egypt.

Philip, Peter, Paul, John the Baptist and particularly the writer of John's Gospel see Jesus as 'the lamb'. In Isaiah 53, one of the 'servant songs', describes the servant as 'like a lamb that is taken to be slaughtered.'

John, the author of the book of Revelation, also sees Jesus as the lamb, the one who has been killed but who now possesses power and authority and is to be worshipped and adored for ever and ever.

Prophet, priest and king

Jesus is the prophet, bringing God's message to his people. Jesus is the great high priest, the only one who stands between God and man. Jesus is the king and Lord of the universe. Paul the apostle wrote that at the end of time everyone will kneel to submit openly to the authority of Jesus.

The World Council of Churches today has for its symbol a ship, often used as a symbol of the church. It was designed by a group of Christians in Germany during Hitler's regime and sent to the Council as a sign of their belief that Christians all over the world are 'all one in Christ Jesus'. The ship afloat on a stormy sea represents the church carrying God's people to safety. The mast makes the sign of the cross. The Greek word *oikoumene* means 'the whole inhabited earth'. So the symbol means 'the total mission of the whole church to the whole of human life and to the whole world'.

3.13 UNDERSTANDING WHY JESUS DIED

In trying to explain to others why Jesus died, the early Christians generally used a variety of pictures or 'images' taken from the Old Testament, the Jewish religion, and everyday life.

Each image or picture was valid. But it is important to understand that no single picture told the whole story. When we think about all the images it helps us to understand the many different yet complementary reasons why Jesus died and what his death means.

Offerings

From the beginning of history people have made offerings to their gods. They have brought a variety of costly sacrifices, including food and drink, birds and animals, to the deity. And they have done so for a variety of reasons. Some have wanted simply to give God a gift. Others have sought through the sacrifice to get close to God. Yet others have tried either by laying down life or releasing it to benefit God or themselves.

Why, in particular, did people kill an animal to make a sacrifice? Perhaps because the life was in the blood and they believed that the taking or giving of life would benefit them in some way, or because they believed that they could transfer their sins to the animal about to die.

Certainly these were some of the reasons which led to sacrifice in Old Testament times. They believed that God was so holy and sin so serious that he could not look at sin. Nothing evil could be allowed to stand in the light of God's presence. But with their sins covered by the sacrificial blood people could enter God's presence. Their sin was blotted out and they knew God's friendship and closeness again.

People felt so helpless and conscious of death that they sought new life. They believed that as the sacrificial blood was poured out so new life was made available.

People were weighed down with the memory of their wrong-doings, so they longed to be set free. And as they transferred their sins onto the head of the animal about to be sacrificed on their behalf they went free.

These vivid pictures of sacrifice came to be applied to the death of Jesus.

The One Offering

Gifts of food and drink and animal sacrifices had to be made over and over again. They could not take away sin and set people free once and for all.

So it was that Jesus became the one, true, living sacrifice. He shed his blood for all people. Offering up himself, laying down his life, he took away the sins of the world.

The result

Christians speak of the death of Jesus as making 'atonement' and achieving 'reconciliation'.

Because of the death of Jesus, God and his people are 'at one' again. This is the way God intended it from the beginning of creation.

Because of the death of Jesus, God and his people are 'reconciled'. When two people who have quarrelled make it up again they are said to be reconciled. So, through the death of Jesus we are reconciled to God, God to us and all of us to one another. We are ready to make a new start.

Pictures of the death of Jesus

Sacrifice Jesus sacrificed himself to take away our sins.

Atonement Jesus' death made it possible for God and his people to be 'at one' with each other.

Ransom Like money paid to those who kidnap a rich man's daughter, Jesus 'ransomed' or bought us back from death: he paid the price for our freedom.

Redemption We 'redeem' special-offer coupons by swapping them for goods at a supermarket or sending them in for something. In the time of Jesus, slaves could be 'redeemed' if the price was paid for their freedom. Jesus' death was the price paid for our freedom.

Justification When in the law-courts a person is 'justified' he is declared innocent and allowed to go free. Because Jesus has paid our death penalty we are declared innocent and set free — we are justified.

Victory over evil While there is sin and death, the power of evil seems in control. But by his death and rising again, Jesus has taken away the power of death itself. One day this victory will be seen publicly by all.

The death of Jesus is not simply an event that happened long ago. Christians believe that it is an event that can change the way we live now.

What the death of Jesus wins

Forgiveness Because Jesus has died for our sin, we can be forgiven.
Communion Because Jesus has broken down the barrier of sin between people and God we can come to God in prayer and praise and experience friendship with him.

JESUS CRUCIFIED

Right The crucifixion of Jesus has been used again and again by artists since the event itself. They see the death of Jesus as an event that helps us to understand God, the world, suffering, and ourselves. These bronze doors from Italy date from the twelfth century.

Left Fourteenth century stained glass from York, England.

Below A mosaic of the crucifixion in a Greek monastery.

Below Jesus is seen crucified between the two thieves in this painting by James Tissot.

Left In this German crucifixion, Jesus is symbolized as the fountain of new life.

Left A twelfth century gold crucifix from Germany.

Below A wall painting (or 'fresco') of the crucifixion from Assisi, in Italy.

Above This icon of the crucifixion is set in the altar screen of a Greek monastery.

Left A statue at Willen Priory in England.

The death of Jesus was no accident or cruel twist of fate. It was planned by God. Jesus often spoke about his death as something he had come to do:

'As Moses lifted up the bronze snake on a pole in the desert, in the same way the Son of Man must be lifted up, so that everyone who believes in him may have eternal life' (John 3:14-15).

'I am the good shepherd, who is willing to die for the sheep' (John 10:11).

'When I am lifted up from the earth, I will draw everyone to me' (John 12:32).

'No one takes my life away from me. I give it up of my own free will' (John 10:18).

'The greatest love a person can have for his friends is to give his life for them' (John 15:13).

'The Son of Man also came not to be served but to serve, and to give his life as a ransom for many' (Mark 10:45).

The faith of the early Christian community sprang from belief in the death and resurrection of Jesus. The two events cannot be separated. And this belief depends upon what God did in the death and resurrection of Jesus. Everything depends on God; nothing depends on us.

It was God who intervened in the Easter experience of the disciples. They were broken people after the crucifixion — but in their time of utter failure God broke in to their lives through the Easter experience, and unexpectedly and powerfully transformed them.

Other Christians after them also had an experience, their own experience of faith in the risen Jesus. They learned to express it in the words:

● **'I believe in** what God did in Jesus' death and resurrection.'
● **'I believe that** Jesus died and rose again.'

A favourite phrase of Pope John Paul II to describe Christians is 'an Easter people'. Christians are 'an Easter people' because they can experience in their own lives the power of the risen Christ, their living Lord, day by day. And Sunday by Sunday they celebrate and give thanks for their new life in broken bread and poured-out wine.

For the first Christians the death and resurrection of Jesus emphasized that their salvation came from outside themselves: it was an act of God. It had not come from within the nation. It had not come as a result of keeping the Law. It had not come from their own faithfulness to God. So too, Christians today look beyond themselves for their liberation, far outside the sphere of their own good and bad behaviour, to God's act of love in Jesus Christ.

Janani Luwum, Archbishop of Uganda, was murdered by the security forces of Idi Amin in 1977 for his faith. His funeral was a time of grief — but also of great joy. Christians look beyond death to a far richer life than we have now.

3.15 JESUS IS COMING AGAIN

One of the most popular prayers of the early Christians was *'Maranatha'*. It meant 'Our Lord come!' Most of them expected the return of Jesus within their lifetime. After all, he had promised them he would return one day.

Testament says, that it is really going to happen.

The first coming of Jesus was as real as any other fact of history (and better attested than most). His second coming was promised along with other promises which have stood the test of time in the experience of millions of people worldwide. Many Christians believe that it too will be a fact of history.

Waiting and watching

But as time passed and Jesus didn't come they began to concentrate on the present. Jesus was present with his people by the Holy Spirit whom he had promised, giving them the power of his risen life. And they remembered that Jesus himself said to his disciples that no one knew when the Son of Man would come back to earth, not even the Son, only the Father.

For this reason they were to be continually on the lookout, alert and watchful.

The Christian hope

Christians believe that one day Jesus will return, as he promised, to complete the work he announced and made possible at his first coming.

Down the centuries there have been plenty of crazy or misguided people who thought Jesus was going to set up his kingdom and return at a particular time or place. But Jesus himself said that no one knows the time or place of his coming. We do not know *when*: but we do know, the New

A new heaven and earth

Jesus came to announce a new kingdom where God, not evil, reigns; a whole new creation where everything will be made new.

He made it possible by dying to take away the sin and death of the old creation. He rose again as the first person, the 'prototype' of the new creation.

Those who trust him, the New Testament says, share this new life, the life of the Spirit, eternal life, already. But they still live in the 'old' world as well! If they die, they are taken out of the realm of time altogether: they go to meet Jesus face-to-face where they experience the total renewal that one day will come to the whole creation.

The chrysalis knows nothing of what it will be like to be a butterfly. In the same way, we cannot know what the new age will be like. The Christian hope is the 'resurrection of the *body*'. We won't be ghosts or disembodied spirits or souls floating in space! But we know that sin and death and suffering will be no more, and everything will be 'made new'.

Jesus said, 'It will be like a man who goes away from home on a journey and leaves his servants in charge, after giving to each one his own work to do and after telling the doorkeeper to keep watch. Be on guard, then, because you do not know when the master of the house is coming — it might be in the evening or at midnight or before dawn or at sunrise. If he comes suddenly, he must not find you asleep. What I say to you, then, I say to all: Watch!'
Mark 13:34-37

A WAY OF LIVING

Mags Law

What is a Christian?

Here are some of the answers we had when we asked this question in a school:

'Someone who goes to church.'

'Someone who leads a good life and cares for other people.'

'Someone who believes the Bible.'

'You're a Christian if your parents are Christians.'
'Someone who believes in God.'

'Someone who is a follower of Jesus.'

'Someone who... well, if you're born in a Christian country, I suppose, I mean, if you're not a Hindu, or a Muslim, for example.'

4

Sections 1-3 tell us something about what Christians believe about the world and about Jesus. This section looks at how Christians live, and what difference their beliefs make to their everyday life.

In most countries there is one religious group (Christians or Muslims, for example) which is larger than any other group. This sometimes leads people to say that, for example, Norway is a 'Christian' country, or Pakistan is a 'Muslim' country.

This may not mean that everyone in that country is a Christian, or a Muslim, but simply that most people, if you asked them, would say that they belong to that religion. Or it may mean that it is the 'official' religion of that country. Sometimes it means that the laws of the country are based on the beliefs of that particular religion. Most people like to feel they belong to a particular religion, but it does not always mean that they believe strongly enough to try to live out their religious beliefs from day to day.

Many countries profess Christian faith, but are torn apart by war and violence. This statue of Christ is in Angola in Africa.

Who are these Christians?

'Christians' was a nickname given to the first disciples of Jesus. It meant 'a follower (or disciple) of Jesus, the Christ' — someone who had put their faith in Jesus, and who tried to live by his teachings. The book of Acts in the Bible tells the story of those early Christians. If there had been newspapers then here are some of the headlines you might have read:

Mob attacks Jason's house
(Read Acts 17:1-9)

Paul claims he was 'blinded by the truth'
(Read Acts 21:37-22:16)

Hearing due tomorrow, as lame man jumps for joy!
(Read Acts 3:1-10 and Acts 4:1-10)

2,000 years on . . . somewhere in Africa

The crowd is hushed as they watch the young man step forward to the edge of the river. He wades out to the man waiting waist-deep in the slow-moving water, turns to stand beside him and places his hands together as if praying.

The older man puts his arm behind the young man's shoulders to support him and lowers him, quickly but gently, backwards beneath the water.

As he comes up out of the water the crowd on the river bank bursts into song. The young man splashes out of the water, smiling broadly as he shakes the water from his hair. He has been baptized. In front of his friends and fellow-Christians he has stated publicly that he is starting a new life — as a follower of Jesus.

Meanwhile . . .

In another church the scene is very different. Angels and saints in stained glass look down on Ian and Gill as they step to the front of the church. Gill holds Ruth, their young baby, in her arms. Two of their friends are with them, to act as godparents to Ruth.

The minister takes Ruth in his arms. He asks Ian and Gill these questions:

Do you turn to Christ?
Do you repent of your sins?
Do you renounce evil?

Ian and Gill, having answered these questions, have to declare publicly their Christian faith and promise to bring up their child 'to fight against evil and to follow Christ'. The godparents promise to help them to do this. The minister makes the

A young man is baptized by immersion in an African river. His baptism is a public sign of his belief in Jesus Christ.

Why repent?

Why do we need to 'turn from evil' to lead a Christian life? We are part of a fallen world — a world gone wrong, full of frustration and self-centredness, a world in a mess. It is not enough just to clean up the environment, or give people a better education or better housing. The problem is 'within us', Jesus said.

'For from the inside, from a person's heart, come the evil ideas which lead him to do immoral things, to rob, kill, commit adultery, be greedy, and do all sorts of evil things; deceit, indecency, jealousy, slander, pride and folly — all these evil things come from inside a person and make him unclean.' (Mark 7:21-22)

So any answers must take account of this basic fact of human nature. Christians believe that marxist or humanist views of how to change people and change society are not radical enough. They are not realistic about what people really are.

66 "Suppose one of you has a hundred sheep and loses one of them — what does he do? He leaves the other ninety-nine sheep in the pasture and goes looking for the one that got lost until he finds it. When he finds it, he is so happy that he puts it on his shoulders and carries it back home. Then he calls his friends and neighbours together and says to them, "I am so happy I found my lost sheep. Let us celebrate!" In the same way, I tell you, there will be more joy in heaven over one sinner who repents than over ninety-nine respectable people who do not need to repent.' 99
Jesus in Luke 15:4-7

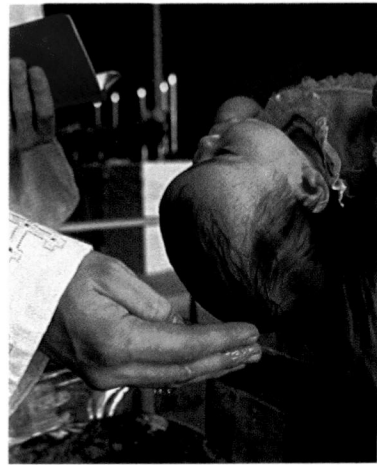

sign of the cross on Ruth's forehead. Then, dipping his fingers into a small bowl of water, he sprinkles the water on her forehead, saying,

'Ruth Elizabeth Powell, I baptize you, in the name of the Father, and of the Son, and of the Holy Spirit. Amen.'

Ruth has only just begun her life but because her parents are Christians, and would like her to grow up as a Christian, she has been baptized.

A public sign

All Christian churches have some sort of public sign that someone has become a Christian — a follower of Jesus. These are just two examples.

In churches where parents bring their children to be baptized (for example, the Roman Catholic, Anglican, or Presbyterian churches) a service of confirmation is held when children are old enough to decide for themselves. In this service, they confirm the promises and beliefs made on their behalf at their baptism by their parents.

In other churches, people are baptized only when they are old

enough to decide for themselves. This is usually called 'believer's baptism' or 'adult baptism'. These churches (for example the Baptist and Brethren churches) often have a service of dedication or thanks-giving for babies and young children from Christian families.

Before confirmation or believer's baptism, there is usually a series of meetings to make sure that the people being baptized or confirmed understand fully what following Jesus means.

Above A Greek Orthodox baptism, where the baby is completely immersed in the water.

It's not magic

Baptism isn't something magical. On its own, it doesn't make someone a Christian. Jesus taught his disciples that what a person was really like inwardly was more important than being religious outwardly.

The Bible uses several pictures to explain what happens when someone decides to follow Jesus. It is like:
● going from a dark room into the sunlight;
● being born all over again;
● being washed clean when you are dirty;
● becoming friends with someone who was once an enemy.

What does baptism mean?

Baptism was first used around the time of Jesus, and Jesus himself was baptized in the river Jordan. Since then, Christians have been baptized in many different ways — some as children, some as adults; some in rivers, or in the sea, and some in churches. It is a public sign to show two things:

● **The person has turned away from doing wrong**, and has been forgiven by God because of the death of Jesus on the cross. The person has been 'washed' and 'made clean' from sin.

● **The person has turned to living for God**. Because of the resurrection of Jesus, a person can share a new 'risen' life, with the help of God's Spirit.

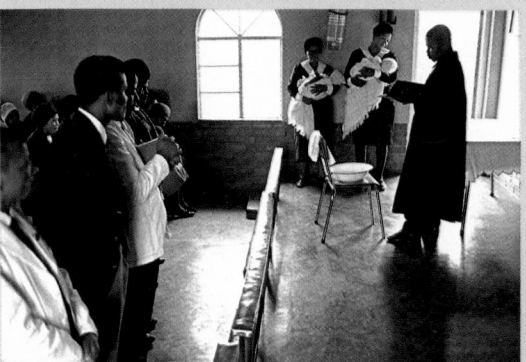

Two babies are baptized in a service in South Africa.

Baptists are so-called because of their belief that people should consciously decide for themselves to be a Christian before being baptized. Their baptism services are often joyful occasions.

Baptism does not have to be a formal event, held in a church. This baptism took place in a local swimming pool.

*Hazel-nut Whirl or
Strawberry Creme?*

The difference

So what difference does it make, being a Christian?

Here are a few replies given by some modern followers of Jesus:

'Many people think a Christian is "someone who lives a good life", but most Christians are more aware of how they fail to live up to Jesus' teachings — and how much they need help.'

'When I began to follow Jesus, I realized that I had to fight to control my temper. I used to get angry with people really easily.'

'I knew, when I became a Christian, that I couldn't go on telling lies and being unkind about other people, so I started to pray for Jesus to help me to tell the truth.'

'I began to realize how selfish I was, how much of my life was centred around what *I* wanted.'

'The Spirit of God reminds me how much God loves me, and that helps me to love other people.'

Life is full of choices!

Some choices are easy. Tidy your room or go to see a film? It's not too difficult to decide!

Sometimes it's more difficult, even when it's not important. Someone passes round a box of chocolates — all those mouth-watering centres to choose from!

Some choices are difficult *and* important. The way we choose may affect our lives for some time. Should I stay on at school? Should I take this job, or try for a different one? Do I want to get married? To him, to her?

Some things we can choose for ourselves; other things are chosen for us by our parents, teachers, friends, or the government of our country. Quite often we don't like what other people choose for us. We prefer to make up our own minds. But then sometimes we cannot decide and so we ask someone else to help us. And all of us find ourselves, at some time, in situations where we don't have any choice — we may *have* to do something, whether we like it or not.

Follow me

Christians have chosen to follow Jesus. That might not sound too difficult. After all, most people admire Jesus, and think his teachings are good. But here is what Jesus said about being his disciple:

'Whoever loves his father or mother more than me is not fit to be my disciple . . . whoever does not take up his cross and follow in my steps is not fit to be my disciple. Whoever tries to gain his own life will lose it, but whoever loses his life for my sake will gain it.'

Jesus made it quite clear to his followers that they must be prepared to die for him, if necessary.

So deciding to follow Jesus is not the sort of choice to make without thinking! The consequences could be serious.

Upside down values

Jesus did not call good people to follow him — he called the bad people! It's the sick who need a doctor, he said, not people already well. Then he showed them how he wanted them to live — by his life, and in what he taught.

In the Sermon on the Mount (see Matthew 5-7) he turned people's ideas upside down. Real happiness is not being rich and successful: even the poor can be rich because they can know God's new rule in their lives. It's those who mourn, those who are humble, those who aim to please God, those who are merciful and pure in heart, those who work for peace or are persecuted because of their faith . . . it's these people who can know true happiness, because they put their trust, not in themselves, but in God.

Jesus taught a life of love to God and to others, a life of trust and prayer.

How much choice do I have . . .

- in the clothes I wear?
- the TV programmes I watch?
- the school I go to?
- my friends?
- what I will eat?
- where I live?
- what subjects I learn at school?
- what I do at the weekend?
- doing what is right (or what is wrong)?
- how I spend my money?

If you don't have much choice over some of these things, who is deciding for you?

What can you do if you disagree with their choice?

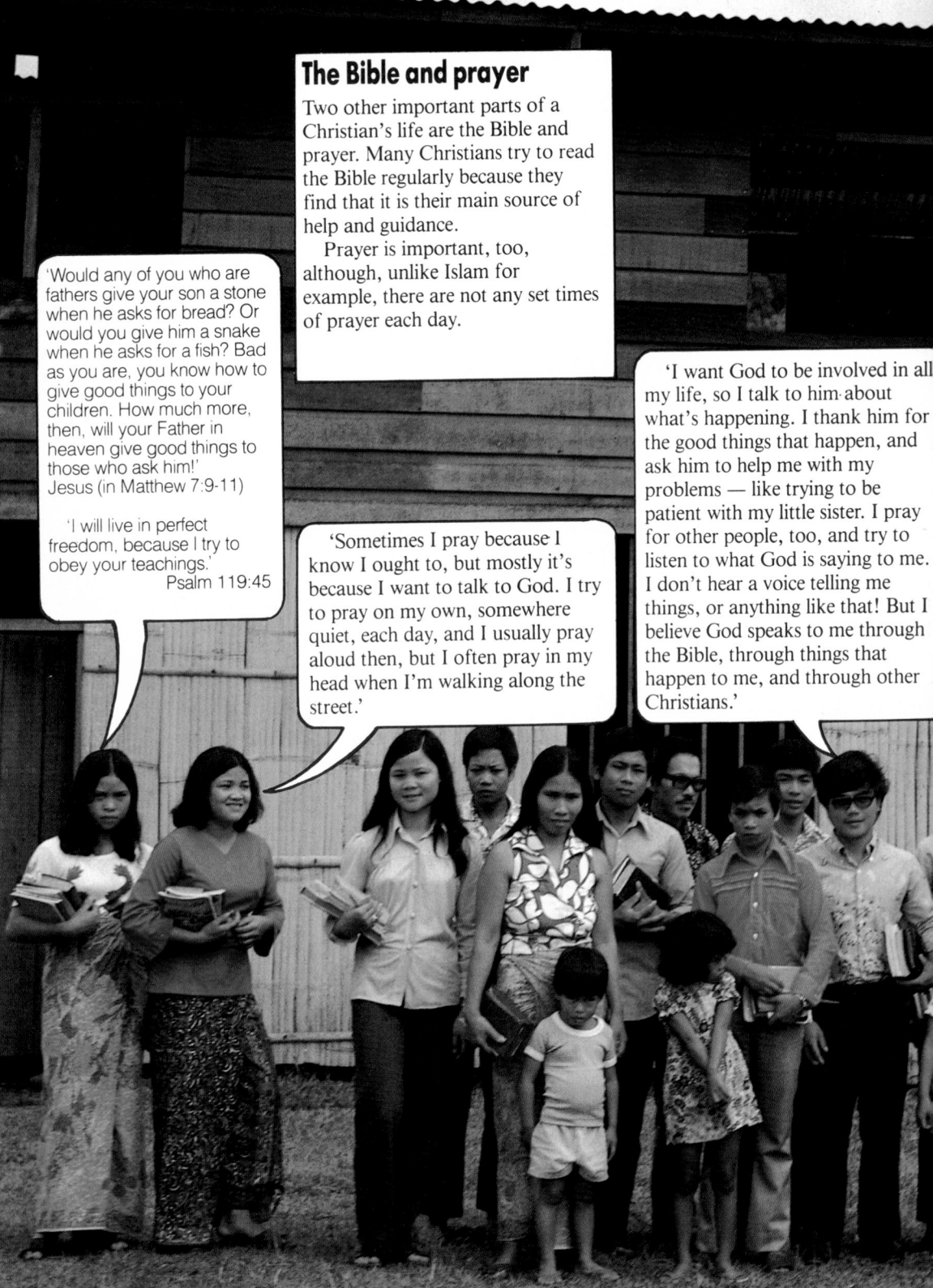

The Bible and prayer

Two other important parts of a Christian's life are the Bible and prayer. Many Christians try to read the Bible regularly because they find that it is their main source of help and guidance.

Prayer is important, too, although, unlike Islam for example, there are not any set times of prayer each day.

'Would any of you who are fathers give your son a stone when he asks for bread? Or would you give him a snake when he asks for a fish? Bad as you are, you know how to give good things to your children. How much more, then, will your Father in heaven give good things to those who ask him!'
Jesus (in Matthew 7:9-11)

'I will live in perfect freedom, because I try to obey your teachings.'
Psalm 119:45

'Sometimes I pray because I know I ought to, but mostly it's because I want to talk to God. I try to pray on my own, somewhere quiet, each day, and I usually pray aloud then, but I often pray in my head when I'm walking along the street.'

'I want God to be involved in all my life, so I talk to him about what's happening. I thank him for the good things that happen, and ask him to help me with my problems — like trying to be patient with my little sister. I pray for other people, too, and try to listen to what God is saying to me. I don't hear a voice telling me things, or anything like that! But I believe God speaks to me through the Bible, through things that happen to me, and through other Christians.'

'You don't have to be a Christian to pray. God listens to everyone. But I think there's something wrong with your attitude to God if you only pray when you're in trouble. It's like never bothering to speak to your friends unless you want to borrow something.'

'Your word is a lamp to guide me, and a light for my path.'   Psalm 119:105

'All scripture is inspired by God and is useful for teaching the truth, rebuking error, correcting faults, and giving instruction for right living, so that the person who serves God may be fully qualified and equipped to do every kind of good deed.'

Paul, writing to Timothy, in 2 Timothy 3:16,17

'It's very easy to think the way everyone else does — like, a few white lies don't really matter, or making unkind jokes about someone behind their back. Reading the Bible helps me to see how Jesus thought about things like that. I don't always find it easy to understand, mind.'

Fruit

Paul also explained how the Holy Spirit could make people more like Jesus. He compares our lives to a fruit tree. With the Holy Spirit at work, the tree would produce fruit: love, joy, peace, patience, kindness, goodness, faithfulness, humility, and self-control.

So when they ask for his help, God gives the followers of Jesus both the wisdom to choose what is right, and the strength to carry it through.

We all pray — even if it is only at the really difficult moments of our lives. Christians believe that prayer can be much more than an emergency phone call to God for help. Prayer can help us to know and love God, and to receive his guidance in the choices we make.

A helper

In stressing new attitudes and values, Jesus did not contradict the Old Testament Ten Commandments (see Section 1). He showed how underneath the law against murder, for instance, lay an attitude — anger can lead to murder, given the opportunity. So again, the root trouble is inside us.

We usually know what is right and wrong. The trouble is doing it. We have a bias towards evil. Even the great early Christian Paul showed how rules of right and wrong were not strong enough by themselves: he wrote, 'I don't do the good I want to do; instead, I do the evil that I do not want to do' (see his letter to the Romans, chapter 7).

This is where Jesus comes in:
● He forgives us our sin.
● He gives us a new life, a new quality of life, 'eternal life'.
● And he gives us a 'Helper' — the Spirit of God, or the Holy Spirit, to give us power to live as God wanted us to.

'The Helper, the Holy Spirit, whom the Father will send in my name, will teach you everything and make you remember all that I have told you.'
Jesus in John 14:26

'But when the Holy Spirit comes upon you, you will be filled with power, and you will be my witnesses.'
Jesus in Acts 1:8

What's important?

How we behave is often influenced by what other people, especially friends, expect of us.

The way that the different Christian churches expect their members to behave varies around the world:

In the Catholic church, members are expected to go to Confession and attend Mass.

In some churches, women and girls are expected to have their heads covered during church services.

In the Salvation Army, members have a uniform which makes them easily recognizable.

Members of the Eastern Orthodox churches may have an 'icon' (a special picture of Jesus, or part of the gospel story) in their homes and say prayers in front of it each morning and evening.

Some of these things have a religious point or historical reason for them. Others simply reflect the culture in a particular part of the world. They are not as important as the inward changes which all the churches teach. These are the things we cannot see so easily — such as attitudes to other people, love and care for others, forgiveness, honesty, or faith.

Everything that church leaders and members do together should be aimed at helping and encouraging each other to live as true followers of Jesus, and to reach out to people outside the church, or those who are members in name only.

Here is how one person described it:

'When we talk about reaching out to people who don't believe, we don't mean going and preaching to them (though we do that sometimes). We want to share the good news that Jesus brought, through showing them that we care for them, as Jesus does. So, if an old lady down the road has got a burst pipe in her house, I don't go down and pray with her — I get Pete, who's a plumber, to come with me, and we fix the pipe! We might well start to talk about God over a cup of tea afterwards, if she wants to. Jesus didn't just talk to people all the time; he healed the sick, fed those who were hungry, and gave them love in his actions as well as his words. That's what we try to do.'

To be a Christian does not mean to have a religious part of our lives. Rather, the whole of life — everything we do — is affected by our relationship with God.

Mother Maria

Mother Maria Skobtsova was a nun in the Russian Orthodox church. In the Second World War, she and her friends helped to hide and protect Jews who were being hunted by the Nazi Secret Police. Because of this, she was arrested and sent to a concentration camp at Ravensbrück in 1943.

Her faith in Christ, and her willingness to take suffering upon herself in order to relieve the pain of others, inspired and encouraged everyone around her in that camp. The prisoners were faced continually with the threat of the gas chambers, and never knew which day might be their last.

On Good Friday, 1945, near the end of the war, a group of prisoners were due to be sent to the gas chamber.

It's hard for us to imagine the relief of those who had not been 'selected' — the feeling that at least while they lived there was some hope. Mother Maria was one of these, yet when she saw the despair and fear in the faces of those who were facing death, she quickly and quietly changed places with one of them, and went to her death in the gas chambers. She was following in Christ's footsteps — giving her life freely because he had given his life for her.

4.3 FAMILY AND FRIENDS

Athletes experience a sense of togetherness when they compete alongside — and against — other athletes. The Olympic Games can be a display of human togetherness on a vast scale.

How do you relate?

Do you feel alone in the world? Or part of the human family? Or simply a member of your own family?

Here are some levels at which each of us relates to others:

● **Immediate family** (Or 'nuclear' family — the family nucleus). Mother, father, brother, sister.

● **Extended family** Uncles, cousins, aunts, second-cousins-twice-removed . . .

In the last century, extended families were usual. But in the Western world today, relatives tend to be more distant, and have a smaller role to play.

● **Friends** Friendships at home or school or through common interests (or perhaps by writing to a penfriend).

● **Team** A sports team is a tightly-knit group of people who train together to achieve a particular sporting aim.

● **Community** A school is a community; so is a local neighbourhood, or a tribe, or a village or town. Or it can be a small community of people who live together like an extended family, sharing homes or possessions.

● **Country or nation** In recent years there has been a surge of 'national consciousness', of feeling proud to belong to a particular country. When it becomes 'nationalism', the pride becomes unhealthy, putting *our* nation above others.

● **Group of nations, or continent** People in Africa, say, or Europe, or Asia, have a sense of belonging

Above and above right The differences between a Western family and a Third World family are obvious. Yet the family relationships are basically the same. Despite our differences of race, wealth and culture, we are all part of the human family.

with others in the same continent. But the more remote the relationship, the less the loyalty the individual has to the wider groups. Many French people would say they are French before saying they are European.

● **Race** With movements of population, different races are not now just identified with particular countries. A 'multi-racial' society is one where people of different racial backgrounds have become *one community*; if they inter-marry, they become *one family*. If the racial groups are not 'integrated', they may live as separate racial communities within *one country* or even a *group of nations*. At what level do you feel related to those of other racial backgrounds?

● **The world family** How many of us feel ourselves citizens of the world, with a common identity with other citizens from every continent? Organizations such as the United Nations and the Olympic Games have all attempted

(not always successfully in the case of the latter!) to make us members of mankind, not just members of our own country.

Getting related

Christianity is about 'getting related'. Christians believe that people were created by God to have 'fellowship' (a common life) with others, and above all with God.

The coming of sin into the world spoilt relationships, as it has spoilt everything else. It has cut us off from our natural relationship with God. It has made for bitterness between people and war between nations.

We are meant to make relationships at every level — but not use them to exclude others.

● Being a member of a family is not supposed to be selfish, cutting us off from others, enjoying only the family unit. We should also have relationships with others.

● Having friendships with others is not supposed to be exclusive, shutting other people out of our lives.

● Being of one nation or one race is not supposed to make us feel superior — or inferior to other nations or races. We may be different from the majority. But we are no better or worse because of the chemistry of our skin. Each race has different strengths.

Our Father

When Jesus came he took up an idea that had been little used before in the Jewish Scriptures, the Old Testament. God is not only our Maker and our Ruler. He can also be our Father.

Jesus came to announce a new start for a world gone wrong. The advance party for his kingdom is a community of people called the church. One day the whole world will be put right: relationships will be mended. In the meantime the church is a community where we can share the new life with others, and where we can work to put relationships right, here and now.

We will be explaining the idea of the church more fully in Section 6. It is:

● **A new family** Just as we are born into a human family, so we can be spiritually re-born into the new family of God, the Christian family. We are brothers and sisters with other Christians.

● **A new community** We can share a common life with people of every nation and every language. There is no barrier now 'in Christ' between God's chosen people of Old Testament days, the Jews, and others, non-Jews. There is no barrier between different races and nations, or between rich and poor. It is to be a loving, sharing community.

Sharing

The followers of Jesus were encouraged to open their houses to strangers and to share their belongings with the needy. To be able to offer hospitality to others was seen as a gift, like being able to teach or preach. Many Christians today open their houses for other Christians to meet, by fostering children, or simply by making their homes welcoming, for people to 'drop in'.

The Christian family has had, and will have, like any family, its arguments and differences. It is divided by differences of tradition and culture, but underneath these differences is a common faith in, and loyalty to, Jesus. Where the differences and divisions lead to totally un-Christian behaviour such as anger and bitterness, or even violence, which contradict the love of Jesus, it is ceasing to be Christian.

Often questions of race, or tribal loyalty, or nationalism, are bound up with religion. Christianity becomes the badge of one of the warring groups. But this is not real Christianity. The dispute arises out of the racial or national loyalties, not from the teaching of Jesus, who said, 'Love your neighbour as yourself'.

❝ One of the people outside said to Jesus, 'Look, your mother and brothers are standing outside, and they want to speak with you.'
Jesus answered, 'Who is my mother? Who are my brothers?' Then, he pointed to his disciples and said, 'Look! Here are my mother and my brothers! Whoever does what my Father in heaven wants him to do is my brother, my sister, and my mother.'
Matthew 12:47-50

Then Peter came to Jesus and asked, 'Lord, if my brother keeps on sinning against me, how many times do I have to forgive him? Seven times?'
'No, not seven times,' answered Jesus, 'but seventy times seven.'
Matthew 18:21-22

Peter said, 'Look! We have left our homes to follow you.'
'Yes,' Jesus said to them, 'and I assure you that anyone who leaves home or wife or brothers or parents or children for the sake of the Kingdom of God will receive much more in this present age and eternal life in the age to come.'
Luke 18:28-29 **❞**

Mount Fuji.

Emiko Sato

Emiko Sato is 19 and lives in Japan. She became a follower of Jesus two years ago, through talking to an American girl, Judy, who was teaching her English. They became friends, and when Judy invited Emiko to come to church with her, she went along.

Japanese people see no reason to believe in only on religion. Most of them are Buddhists but, for example, they recognize Christmas, and give each other presents, and almost everyone takes part in Shint ceremonies throughout their life. So, at first, Emiko was simply curious to find out what Christians believed.

When Emiko became a Christian, she found it hard to explain to her parents that she could no longer join in some of the traditional family customs and festivals, which centre around ancestor worship or praying for good luck at different stages in life.

Emiko's parents worry that she will not revere them when they die, in the way that they honour the memory of their parents and grandparents. Emiko's sister believes she will bring bad luck on the family by following a new religion.

The Japanese people value duty and loyalty above everything, and Emiko now has a new loyalty to Jesus which conflicts with what her parents expect of her. In their eyes, she brings shame on the family just by being different, and not following the customs of ordinary Japanese people. Soon, Emiko will have to face pressure from her parents to make a 'good' marriage, which is very important to them. They will not understand that she would rather marry a Christian, even if, socially, the marriage may be a 'bad' one.

'I wouldn't want to sleep with someone before I get married. I think sex is meant for marriage and I'm happy to learn about sex with the person I get married to. I think friends put a lot of pressure on you, especially boys, to sleep with a girl before you get married.'

'If you sleep with someone and then you split up, it makes things much worse. And it's a really bad start to marriage if you have to get married because a baby is on the way. But if you sleep with one person, and then you split up, why shouldn't you sleep with your next boy or girlfriend? In the end, sex isn't really anything special, and I think that's sad. I think God meant it to be something special that you only share with one person.'

'People get the words "love" and "sex" mixed up. People talk about sexual intercourse as "making love", but they don't really know what love is all about.'

We saw in Section 1 that sex and marriage are part of God's good creation. Sex is built in! We were created to enjoy the relationship of man and woman.

Like other relationships, sex has become warped and spoiled by people's sinfulness. It has become selfish, self-centred, something for 'self-gratification' — pleasing me, in other words!

This is not how God intended it. It is Christianity's joy to show how this part of life can be set free, liberated from its bondage to sin! There is a better way . . .

Back to the roots

When Jesus was asked about marriage, he pointed people back to the beginning. Two people leave their parents and set up a new family unit, a new 'couple', a new home. They become 'one flesh'. They get to know one another, and

enjoy one another's company. Sex both expresses their love and also deepens their relationship.

So people getting married have to be responsible enough to set up their own home. They can't just go on 'depending on mum'. And mum has to let go, too.

The new couple need to be seen by the community as having set up a new home. They 'get married'. They get a bit of paper, a marriage licence to show that the community recognizes their new status.

Then they have to work away at making their marriage work. The romantic dream of 'living happily ever after' is . . . a romantic dream! Getting married is the beginning, not the end, of the story.

The couple's love for one another must be deepened. Their marriage may, in some cultures, have been arranged by parents. In other cultures it may depend only

Christians see marriage as a lifelong commitment to each other. In a world of rocketing divorce rates, to be loved into old age brings great peace and security.

on mutual attraction! Either way, the couple must learn how to love each other, physically and emotionally and practically. So in the Christian view of marriage, sex has a key role to play. Couples express their love, and deepen it at the same time.

Man and woman are equal partners, with different roles, complementing one another. They are living, not just for themselves, but as a new home, a new couple, a new family within the community. They have committed themselves to a lifelong partnership.

Children are conceived and born as part of a loving home. They are not just a nuisance, or a necessary evil. They need a loving, committed relationship.

Alternatives

Today there are many rival views of sex and marriage on offer:

● **Casual sex** Sex is like eating. Enjoy it! Satisfy your appetite. It's not tied in to love or marriage. Snags: This view is purely selfish and so cannot bring lasting fulfilment. It's at the expense of someone else who may be hurt or emotionally harmed. Girls in particular need the security of a loving relationship to learn to be satisfied sexually. There must be a better way!

● **Living together** This is a half-way house. It can be a trial marriage, to see how it goes but without the commitment. Or it can be a short-term arrangement. The snags are that it is neither one thing nor another. There is no 'leaving' parents and home. There is no security, no commitment, so no 'giving' in love. There is no recognition by the community — so nobody knows whether it is a new home, a new social unit, or not . . . And in practice trial marriages are not a real test at all: statistically people who have tried are *more* likely to end up in divorce, not less likely. When 'living together' comes to an end, there is the hurt of pulling apart two people who have become 'one flesh'.

God created us to love and be loved. The love between a man and a woman is one of his greatest gifts to us. As one writer put it, 'God thought of sex first'.

● **Sex is OK if you're loving** In this view, sex is an expression of loving and caring for the other person, as well as physical desire. It's not a question of marriage, or commitment, or leaving parents, or setting up a new home . . . Snags: It's using a means of sealing a relationship which you don't really want to seal, and of expressing love which you may feel now but don't want to commit yourself to long-term.

● **Marriage and sex are a way of getting yourself a home and children** In many societies, the man gets himself a wife to look after him and bear him children. There is no thought of partnership. The woman is part of the man's possessions. Snags: the woman is debased, and there is none of the Bible's ideal of marrying for mutual companionship and help.

When things go wrong

Sadly, marriages go sour. People drift apart. Perhaps it never came

up to the high ideal: the magazines promised us we'd be 'happy ever after', and it was never quite like that . . . The marriage was asked to bear a strain it was never designed for.

The Christian ideal is marriage for life. Nothing else matches up to God's purpose for it. The vows taken in church are for a life-long commitment.

At the same time the Bible recognizes that we are living in a non-ideal world. Divorce was allowed 'because of the hardness of people's hearts'.

So now the church has the difficult job of holding two things together:

● Marriage is a life-long commitment.

● Divorced people, like others who have gone wrong, must be loved and cared for, and given the opportunity for a new start.

I love you

To express the different levels of relationship with others, the Greek language (in which the New Testament was written) used different words.

◆ **Love** or Christian love is something for which a new word had to be found in the New Testament (*agape* in Greek). It depends not on reacting to someone else but on a quality in ourselves. So it is possible to love the squalid, the unattractive, the suffering. Christians are given this sort of love by God's Spirit within them, living out the love Jesus shared when he served people and even died for them.

◆ **Sexual love** or erotic love (*eros* in Greek) is 'being in love', love between the sexes. We respond to somebody attractive, or to something about another person which arouses us.

◆ **Affection** is love between parents and children, or fondness of brothers and sisters (yes, really!).

◆ **Friendship** is when people are good companions, or 'kindred spirits' — 'just good friends' rather than 'boyfriends' or 'girlfriends'.

4.5 THE WORLD OF WORK

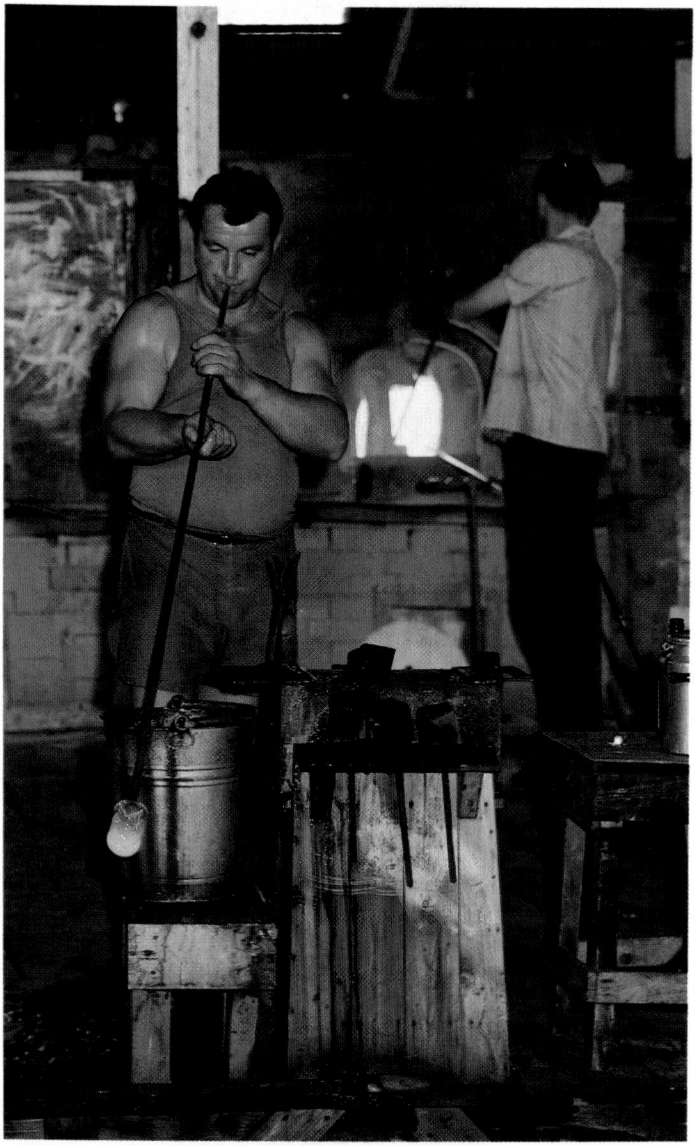

Work plays an important part in our lives. Our enthusiasm for it, or our boredom with it will affect everything else we do. ***Below*** *A glassblower at work.* ***Right*** *Roughnecks making up a new joint of pipe on an oil rig.*

We have already seen in Section 1 that God made us with a role to play in the world he created:

- to manage the world's resources;
- to do creative work, just as God created;
- to use our talents and gifts;
- to enter into God's 'vocation' for our lives.

How have Christians related this to the world of work?

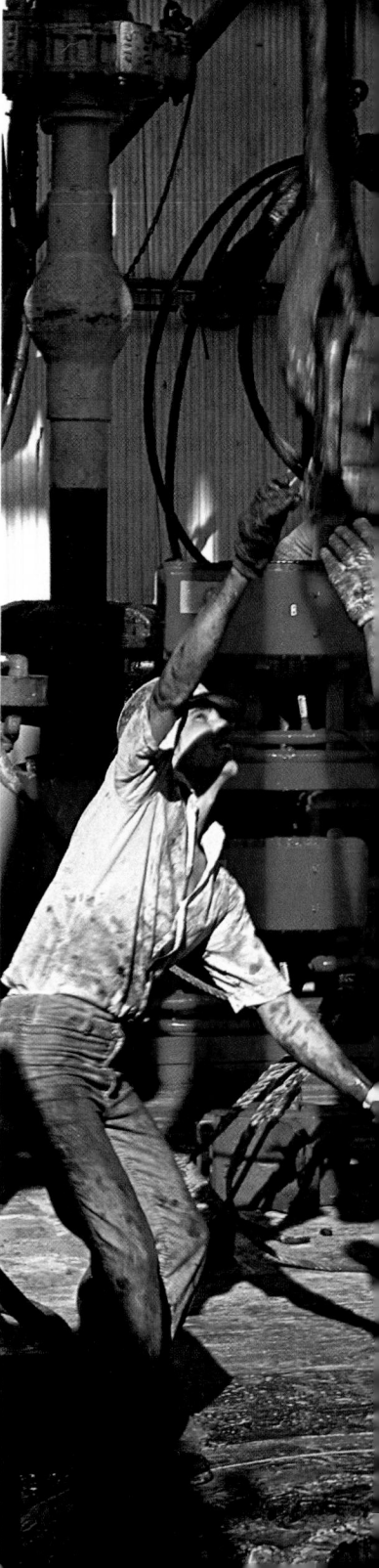

Models of society

Over the years different groups have adopted different 'models' of their role in society and the world of work. Which do you think is most in agreement with what God intended us to do?

● **Self-sufficiency** I will bake my own bread, make my own clothes, grow my own food, teach my own children, generate my own electricity . . .

● **Community** One person will bake the bread, another make the clothes, another grow the food, another teach the children, another build a power station . . . Money is the way of exchanging goods and services. Those with work will pay for the unemployed.

● **Capitalism** People will work for me making goods that others will buy. So there will be work for people. By making lots of clothes cheaply I will raise the quality of life for a lot more people. I will be creating wealth or employment or both.

● **Labour** All I have is my muscle, my mind. I will sell my labour to the highest bidder. What matters is not what I do but the money I earn to support my family and give me a good standard of living.

● **Craftsmanship** My job satisfaction will be in creativity, in my artistry. I will make beautifully designed, handmade clothing that will give pleasure to people, and hopefully earn enough to live at the same time . . .

● **Escape** The world is evil, work is a rat-race. Unions and employers are fighting . . . I will opt out of the sinful world and work for the poor, or live a life of prayer.

● **Money-making** I will work to make money. I will set up a business that will give maximum return so that I can do well for myself, my family and charitable

Money, money, money

What do you spend your money on?
    clothes
    food, sweets and drink
    hobbies or sports
    records or cassettes
    magazines and books
    entertainment (cinemas, discos etc.)
    travel
    holidays
    charities
    You could try writing down what you think you spend on each of these things each week.
    We all daydream sometimes. Have you ever thought about what you would do if someone gave you a lot of money? How would you spend it?
    What things do you think are more important than money?

'The love of money is a source of all kinds of evil.'
Paul

'The only safe rule is to give more than we can afford.'
C. S. Lewis

'God loves the one who gives gladly.'
Paul

Millionaire gives it all away

Mr Piet Derksen, one of the wealthiest businessmen in The Netherlands, said he was selling his sports equipment business and giving about £107m to finance Third World projects.

A devout Catholic, Mr. Derksen said: 'My wealth has been like a stone round my neck — I'm glad to get rid of it. I could shout with joy.'
Newspaper report, March 1984

causes. I will buy the materials as cheaply as I can in the world, and pay for labour to get things done as cheaply as possible so that I can make maximum profit.

● **Service** I will give my life in the service of others: missionary work, or teaching, or nursing. I will be working, not for money, but for the good of others.

● **Stewardship** I will work for the conservation of nature and protection of resources, and for development projects which ensure the environment is not spoiled.

Vocation

Christians believe that God has a plan for their lives. He calls them to a particular job or service. It may not be to full-time employment — it may be to church work or other jobs in the community, particularly where there is not much employment.

God also gives us 'gifts' or talents to use in his service, both in the church or more generally. Artistic gifts, such as being a poet or painter, are God-given, though not of course given only to Christians. So are abilities such as being good at sport or music.

So there is no separation between 'religious' life and so-called 'secular' life. Christians are called to give every part of their lives to God. They do their work not just to earn a wage or get on in life, but above all to please God in whatever they are doing.

Certain types of work have always been seen as belonging only to men.

And of course they will work in a Christian way — not selfishly, at the expense of others, or by dishonesty or lying or cheating or greed, but caring for others, trying to make good relationships and do a good job of work to the best of their ability.

Tithes and taxes

All through history, communities have always needed money for things which do not earn money. In the Bible, people gave a tenth of their income, a 'tithe', for the upkeep of the priests and religious services.

Governments raise taxes to pay for services which the community needs to share. So schools or hospitals, for instance, can be paid for either by charging for each school place or hospital bed (the 'private' system), or by sharing the cost over the whole community by means of taxes.

So tax evasion is obviously wrong. It is a way of trying to get out of our share of the cost of community spending. (Tax 'avoidance' is not wrong if it means not paying taxes we don't have to pay!)

In democratic countries, how government spends our money is decided in the nation's budget. Many Christians do not like the share of the budget spent on arms, for instance. Some propose not paying that proportion of our taxes. But the democratic way is to try to vote for a government and affect its decisions in a way that will get the money spent on good social services rather than war.

Microchips, satellite communications, and a host of expanding technologies have changed the face of work. But will this mean jobs for more people — or less?

'You cannot serve both God and money.'   Jesus

'Do not store up riches for yourselves here on earth, where moths and rust destroy, and robbers break in and steal. For your heart will always be where your riches are.'   Jesus

Money brings happiness — true or false?

Here's what some people thought when we asked them:

False — because it makes you selfish; you just want more money and more things.

True — because you can make life very comfortable and have lots of fun.

False — because a person's true life isn't made up of the things he owns, however rich he is.

True — because you can be generous to your friends and make a lot of people happy.

False — unless you give it all away, because you're having a good time while other people are dying of starvation.

What do you think?

One of the statements above was said by Jesus. Do you know which one it is?

A man checks the quality of a plate at a porcelain factory in France.

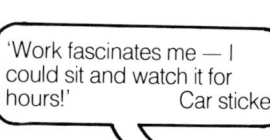

'Work fascinates me — I could sit and watch it for hours!'   Car sticker

Assembling watch bracelets in a German watch factory.

On the make

In the New Testament, a man called Zacchaeus had the job of collecting taxes for the occupying force, the Romans. So he was despised and unpopular because he would also fiddle the taxes, lining his own pocket at the same time.

Then Jesus called him . . .

What did Zacchaeus have to do to put things right? You can read his story in Luke 19:1-10.

The tent-maker

Like his master, Jesus, who was a carpenter by trade, Paul earned his living wherever he went on his missionary travels. He was a 'tent-maker', or leather-worker.

He was also concerned that Christians put their love for one another into practice. When Jewish Christians were suffering hardship because of famine, he organized a collection from non-Jewish Christian churches. It was a practical way of showing solidarity.

Christians on money

'I think you should be content with what you have, but I don't think there's anything wrong with being rich. Jesus just said it's harder for well-off people to see their need of God.'

'The main thing Jesus taught about money was how to give it away! I believe I should give at least a tenth of what I earn to charity. I give mine to Christians working in poorer countries, and to people I know who are doing work to serve God, which they aren't getting paid for.'

'Money's no good to you when you die, is it?'

'I think it's important that, however much money you have (or haven't), got, you should use it in a way that shows that you love God, and you care about other people who are worse off than you.'

Working out a problem in the computer room.

4.6 LIVING IT OUT

Christians celebrate their faith on Pentecost Sunday in Dublin, Ireland. The Christian faith is not a private affair. It is good news for all people — and good news has to be shared.

Love — and justice

When I was at graduate school my landlord and landlady for two years were black Americans. I sat with them the night Martin Luther King was killed. After that time I lived in the black inner city, and most of what I know about oppression I learnt first hand from black Americans.

Most important of all to me was the Scriptures. As I tried to listen to what they were saying I discovered they contain an enormous amount of material about justice.
Ron Sider, author of *Rich Christians in an Age of Hunger.*

The first Christians were a tiny minority group. The Jews were against them — for they claimed that the promised Messiah had actually come in the person of Jesus. The Romans put up with them — until they claimed a higher allegiance than Caesar. The result was often trouble: unpopularity or worse.

Since then, the church has grown world-wide. Yet Christians in many parts of the world are still a minority. In many Western countries, the church has declined to the point where Christians are a small minority in a pagan society. Elsewhere, in countries such as South America, Africa, Indonesia and Korea, there has been enormous growth.

Whether in a minority or not, Christians have the job of living out their faith: in their own personal lives; in their family; in their community; in their work; possibly in public life.

We all talk about the things that excite us — the football score, a girl or boyfriend, your favourite band. Christians talk about Jesus because he means so much to them.

Personal lifestyle

Jesus lived a life of love, caring for others and thinking nothing of his own comfort. He also lived for what was right, putting God's way at the centre. And he lived a life of devotion, withdrawing to pray, depending on his heavenly Father from day to day.

In the same way Christians are called to be loving, concerned, praying people.

Love, as we have seen, is not just a warm feeling. It is a God-given spur to action among the poor, the down-and-outs, the needy. A Christian will ask: who are the needy in *my* area? How can I live to serve others rather than just trying to please myself?

The Christian in the community

Down the centuries, Christians have been in the forefront of caring ministries, in helping those in need. They have been concerned for education, introducing schools as part of their missionary outreach. They have been concerned for people who are ill or without medical help, setting up hospitals and working to cure diseases such as leprosy, or looking to God for direct healing as a sign of his coming kingdom.

Today Christians are working in the slums, like Mother Teresa in Calcutta or missionaries in Manila. Or they may be working in famine relief, or helping in projects to help build agriculture or develop Third-World industries.

In local communities, too, there is always need for people who will get involved in caring projects: helping the elderly and the shut-ins, for instance.

In all this, Christians are living out their new life. It is not a duty, trying to earn a way to heaven. It is a loving response to God's love, a sharing of the good news of the gospel, working out in practice the new life given by God's Spirit.

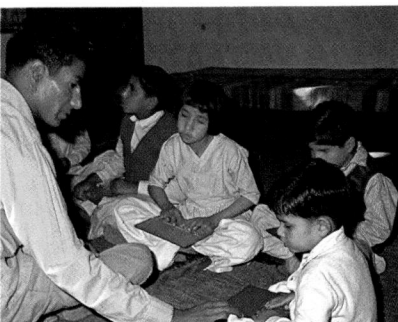

Christian love is not just talked about; it shows itself in action. Here a Christian teacher teaches blind children to read braille in Pakistan.

Mother Teresa of Calcutta was awarded the Nobel Peace Prize in 1979 for her work among the outcasts and dying in India. In her Home for the Dying, many of the poorest people are welcomed and cared for, for the first time in their lives.

Meet hate with love

On 1 December 1955 Rosa Sparks quite unintentionally started a chain of events that involved thousands of people across the United States. She broke the law, not by attacking someone, or stealing something, but by refusing to give up her seat on the bus!

Rosa was black, and in her town the law said that black people should give up their seats to white people if the bus was full. Rosa knew that her legs ached just as much as anybody else's, white or black, and she refused.

On the day of her trial, black people boycotted the town's buses — a very effective protest as the buses were only a quarter full as a result. They stayed that way for 382 days, while the local black people walked to work. Eventually, the Supreme Court of the United States ordered that all citizens should have equal rights to seats on the buses.

The leader chosen by the boycotters was a local Baptist minister, Martin Luther King. In the years that followed, he suffered bitter attacks on himself and his family, as well as gaol sentences and misunderstanding from both black and white people, as he campaigned for equality for black Americans. He refused to meet violence with violence.

One night he came home to find that a bomb had exploded outside his house. A crowd had gathered, and there was talk of violent retaliation against the white people of the town. Martin Luther King told the crowd,

66 'If you have weapons, take them home. We cannot solve this problem through violence. We must love our white brothers no matter what they do to us. We must make them know that we love them. Jesus still cries out, "Love your enemies". That is what we must live by. We must meet hate with love.' 99

Not all black Americans were willing to follow Martin Luther King's non-violent path. Many could not meet the bitterness and hatred they experienced from white people with love. Martin Luther King believed that the use of violence would bring a new kind of slavery. Only love could bring freedom.

In 1968, Martin Luther King went to Memphis. He said that when he arrived, 'Some began to talk of what would happen to me from some of our sick white brothers. But it really doesn't matter with me now. I just want to do God's will.'

The next day, he was assassinated as he talked with some friends — a victim of the violent hatred which he had always opposed.

'You are a light for the whole world . . . your light must shine before people, so that they will see the good things you do and praise your Father in heaven.'
Jesus in Matthew 5:14,16

'God is directly concerned in the way men behave to one another — that is, in politics.'
Trevor Huddleston

Christians in communist lands

The Catholic University of Lublin, Poland, recently conducted a study into the beliefs of young people in seven Polish towns. More than 90 per cent of the 1,500 young Poles questioned in the study stated that they were ready to sacrifice their life for their Christian faith. In contrast, less than five per cent were ready to do so for socialist ideals.

In Czechoslovakia, the Institute of Scientific Atheism reports that 'representative sociological surveys' suggest that 51 per cent of Slovaks and 30 per cent of Czechs are religious believers.

Despite six decades of harsh persecution, in the USSR one in three adults has religious beliefs while only 15 per cent claim to be convinced atheists — again according to official estimates.

Politics and social action

Christian people are called to many different jobs, as we have seen. Some will be concerned for good government, and for changing society by political action.

The fight against slavery was pioneered by people whose Christian conscience was stirred. In the last century a group in London called the Clapham Sect were dedicated to the abolition of the slave trade across the world. One of the members was William Shaftesbury, who continued to fight until, in 1833, a law was passed to free all slaves in the British colonies.

In South America today, many poor communities are being exploited by greedy landowners. The church has taken up their cause, caring for the poor and needy against the wealthy and powerful.

Many of the abuses in the world today need Christian action. In the early days of the trades union movement, Christian people took up the cause of workers who were being exploited and who had no voice of their own. Today many of the battles for good pay and good conditions have been won. The Christian voice is needed to work out new ways of bringing peace, productivity and a fair deal in industry.

Changing the world

Christians work to see God's kingdom, God's rule announced in Jesus, come in the lives of people worldwide. So long as we live in a sinful world, the job will never be complete. Jesus promised that he would come back to put into practice fully what he started at his first coming. Then, with the 'new heavens and the new earth', the wrongs of the world will be put right.

Until then, it is the Christian's calling to live as 'salt' in society: stopping it going rotten, bringing taste to it.

And the Christian is to be 'light' in society: letting the light of God's law and the good news of Jesus shine out in their own lives, their communities, and throughout the world.

Rich and poor

Recently, Christians in the wealthier parts of the world have become more aware of the injustice caused by their enjoyment of products obtained at an unjustly low cost from less industrialized countries. 'Fair trading' organizations make available goods from 'poorer' countries at a price which gives the producers a fair reward for their work.

Christians have also begun to see the need for a simpler style of life, which is less centred around possessions, in order to create a more equal distribution of the world's food and materials.

As one Christian says, 'The problem is not that there isn't enough food to go round, but that we are too greedy.'

Why is surplus grain hoarded in rich countries while poor countries are starving? Christians are concerned to combat this injustice.

GOD SPEAKS: THE BIBLE

John Young

Under the soft glow
of oil-lamps, a group of
young people at a camp are
discussing a book...
What is this book with its stories of
primeval times, of love and war
and family sagas?
What is this book with its message of a strange visitor
speaking of love and peace and a new start?
What are these poems and prophecies and
parables which still speak to people today?
What is this message of
hope and liberation?

5

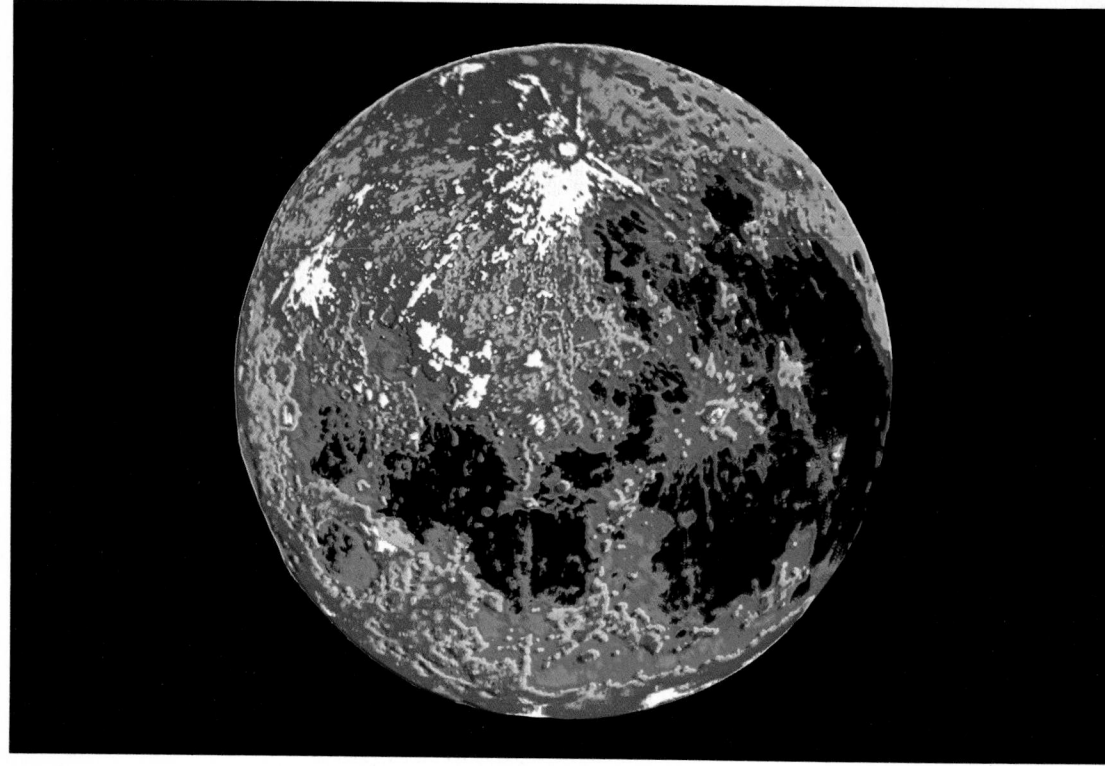

Can the Bible, written so long ago, help us to make sense of the world of today?

'Whoever made this book made me; it knows all that is in my heart.'
A Chinese reader of the New Testament

'The Bible is the cradle in which Christ is laid.'
Martin Luther

Which book has been read by more people than any other book in the history of the world?

Which book gathers more dust on more shelves than any other book?

Which book has proved its power to transform the wicked, guide the bewildered and comfort the dying?

Which book is presented to kings and queens at coronations, to presidents as they are sworn in and to witnesses in courts of law?

Which book claims to be God's message of hope to a world in need?

Only one book. We call it the Bible. It is an ancient book.

It was written by people who could travel no faster than horses or camels could carry them. They had no electricity or gas, no cars or aeroplanes, no newspapers or television.

Why then should we bother with the Bible? How can it help us today?

Jews and Christians give the same answer. The Bible continues to be relevant because:
● It speaks about God: and God doesn't change.
● It speaks about human nature: and human nature doesn't change.

Big questions

The Bible deals with those aspects of human life which remain important, whether we travel by jet or by camel. It examines life's really big questions — questions which we all have to face sooner or later.

Why do innocent people suffer? Is there any real purpose in life? Do we just fizzle out after about seventy years, or is there life after death? Where is God in this great jumble of human activity? Does he exist? Does he care? How can we sort out right from wrong? Is there a recipe for happiness? How should we behave towards other people? When we go wrong, can we be forgiven?

These questions — and many others — are wrestled with in the pages of the Bible. They are not discussed as theory, but worked out in practice in people's lives.

Millions of people have found that the answers given in the Bible are true. The answers are convincing, because they work out in human experience.

Other books deal with these important questions too. But the Bible claims a unique authority. Jews and Christians believe that the ancient authors of the Bible wrote under the inspiration of God's Spirit. In the Bible we read words which were written by men; but the Bible is called 'the word of God', too.

Despite the many changes of the twentieth century, people deep down remain the same. This is why Christians believe that the Bible can be read and used by modern people.

New life in prison

A sixteen-year-old murdered a member of a rival gang in Singapore. He was sentenced to life in prison. He could look forward to nothing but endless days in solitary confinement. But the prisoner in the next cell somehow managed to pass to him ten pages from the Gospel of Luke. From those ten pages he read and re-read the words of Jesus. Slowly he understood, and asked for God's forgiveness.

To his surprise, he was released from prison. Now he is helping ex-prisoners and drug addicts put their shattered lives back together.

Simon Izarra is a Peruvian who was introduced to the Bible by an outburst of temper and a rubbish bin! His teacher tore up a Bible in anger, and threw it away. After the lesson, Simon took the torn-up pages from the wastebin, and read them. He was gripped and convinced by what he read, and now he is a Bible translator.

5.2 A BEST-SELLING LIBRARY

A book worth fasting for

A Russian labour camp is a terrible place — long, cold days, filled with dreary inactivity or very hard work. This is 'life' for a young Russian called Alexander Ogorodnikov. In September 1980, shortly after his marriage to Yolena, Alexander was arrested. He was sent to a labour camp because of his Christian activities.

Sometimes he has to sleep on a concrete floor, covered in filth. He has too few clothes to keep him warm, and he is often ill.

But he is full of courage, and in 1982 he went on hunger strike. One of his demands was that he should see a priest. He also wanted two books to be returned to him. One was his prayer book; the other was his Bible.

A book worth dying for

William Tyndale was an English scholar who longed for a quiet life. He wanted nothing more than to study Greek and Hebrew and to write books. But he was disappointed. His life was full of adventures and narrow escapes.

At last he was captured and condemned. On 6 October 1536 he was strangled. Then his body was burnt. This happened in Belgium, but his execution was welcomed by many important people in England.

William Tyndale's main crime was translating the Bible into English.

If you go to a bookshop and ask for the world's best-selling book, what will they give you? A strange look and a request to be more specific! But if they know the book trade well, they will hand you a Bible.

It is in fact a mini-library, written by about forty different authors. The world 'Bible' means just that — a collection of books. Here are some facts and figures about the world's best-seller.

● It is divided into two large sections: the Old Testament and the New Testament. The word 'testament' means 'covenant' or 'agreement'. It refers to the agreement which God has made with the human race. It describes God's love for the world which he made, and the terms on which we may receive forgiveness and eternal life.

● The Old Testament contains 39 books and covers a period of over 1,000 years. The New Testament contains 27 books and covers about 100 years.

But there is another way of looking at this. The Bible covers every moment of time — and eternity too. It refers back to the 'time' before the world was created; and it looks forward to a 'new heaven and a new earth'.

● Some Bibles contain a third section called 'Deutero-Canonical' books or the Apocrypha. The twelve books in this section contain stories and describe events in the period of time between the Old and the New Testaments. They are not included in the Hebrew Bible. For Protestant Christians these books do not have the same authority as the rest of the Bible, and Bibles are often printed without them.

● Some books in the Bible carry the author's name. The identity of some other authors can be worked out. But several writers are

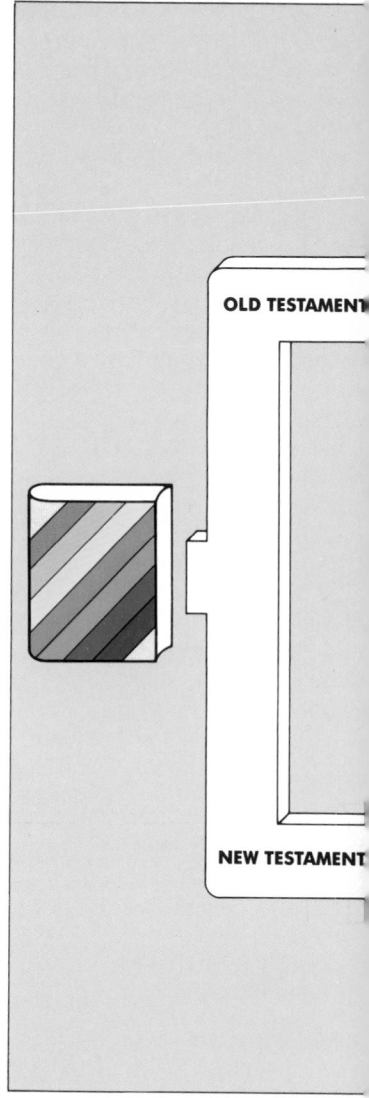

unknown. Some of the books were written by more than one person. Other writers acted as editors — re-working earlier documents, or recording stories passed on by word of mouth.

● There are considerable differences between these authors. Some were learned scholars; others had little formal schooling. Some were historians; others were poets. Some were lawyers; others told stories. Some wrote from high positions in

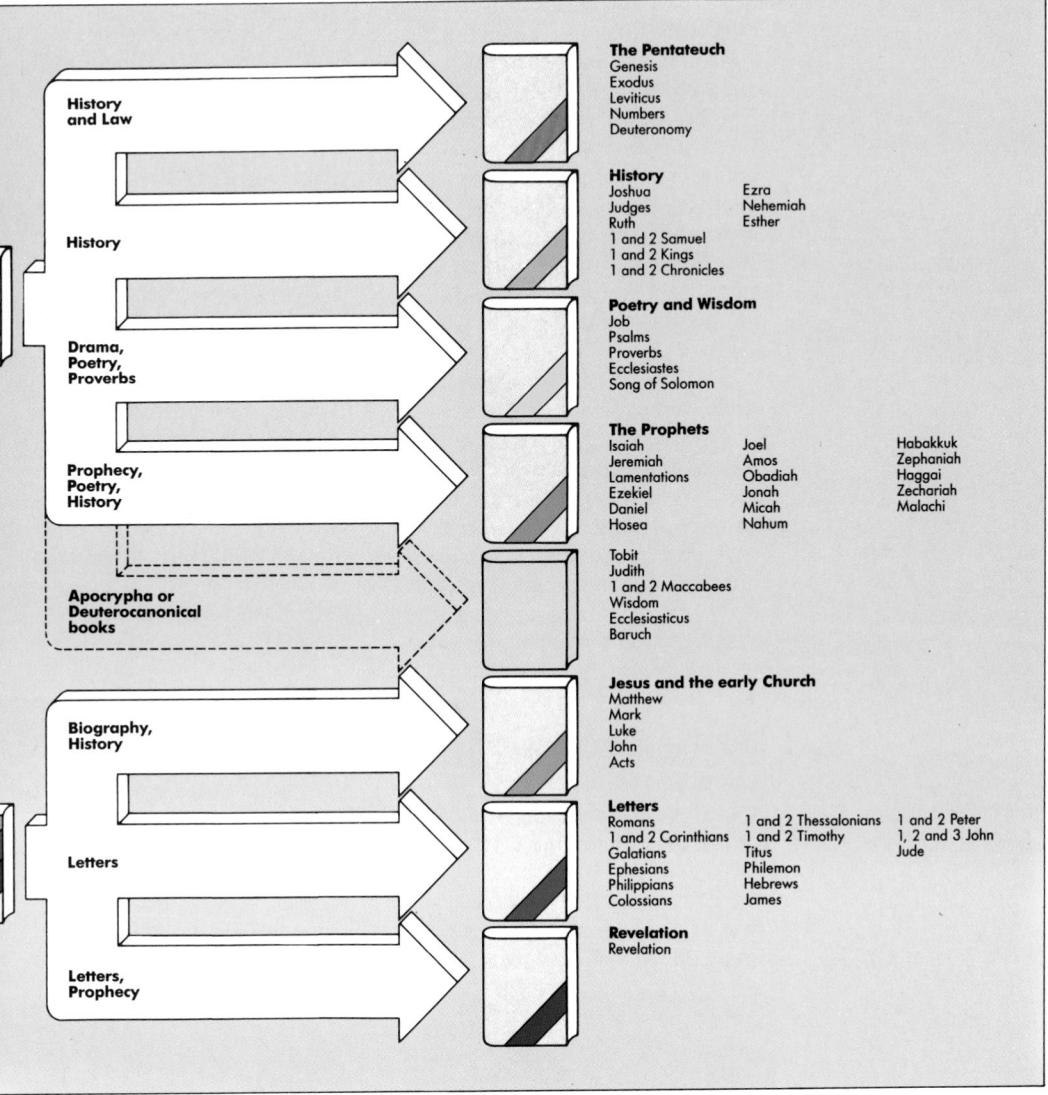

The Pentateuch
Genesis
Exodus
Leviticus
Numbers
Deuteronomy

History
Joshua	Ezra
Judges	Nehemiah
Ruth	Esther
1 and 2 Samuel	
1 and 2 Kings	
1 and 2 Chronicles	

Poetry and Wisdom
Job
Psalms
Proverbs
Ecclesiastes
Song of Solomon

The Prophets
Isaiah	Joel	Habakkuk
Jeremiah	Amos	Zephaniah
Lamentations	Obadiah	Haggai
Ezekiel	Jonah	Zechariah
Daniel	Micah	Malachi
Hosea	Nahum	

Tobit
Judith
1 and 2 Maccabees
Wisdom
Ecclesiasticus
Baruch

Jesus and the early Church
Matthew
Mark
Luke
John
Acts

Letters
Romans	1 and 2 Thessalonians	1 and 2 Peter
1 and 2 Corinthians	1 and 2 Timothy	1, 2 and 3 John
Galatians	Titus	Jude
Ephesians	Philemon	
Philippians	Hebrews	
Colossians	James	

Revelation
Revelation

Labels (left side):
History and Law
History
Drama, Poetry, Proverbs
Prophecy, Poetry, History
Apocrypha or Deuterocanonical books
Biography, History
Letters
Letters, Prophecy

he king's court; others wrote from prison.

Despite all these differences there is a remarkable unity of purpose. Taken together, these writings speak powerfully of the purposes of God for people in every place and every age. Jews and Christians believe that God guided the writers:
● Giving them deep insight;
● Blending the books together to tell a remarkable story.

The Bible is a whole collection of books: stories, laws, prophecy, poetry, history — and even a love song. It is a book that has fascinated — and surprised — its countless readers.

5.3 WHY THESE BOOKS?

Science

Genesis and modern science do not 'agree' or 'disagree' with each other, because they use different types of language, and are concerned with different problems.

Central to this view is the idea that *literal* truth is not the only real truth. We are, in fact, quite used to accepting statements as true, even though we would not dream of taking them literally:
'I lost my head.'
'I smell a rat.'
'She's an old battle-axe.'
'He's got a frog in his throat.'

When Robert Burns wrote 'O my Luve's like a red, red rose' we understand that he did not mean that every embrace was extremely painful, or that her complexion suggested she was prone to nose-bleeds!

Parables and novels can teach profound truths without being *literally* true.

The same approach can be applied to the early chapters of Genesis. We can believe that the writer of Genesis was inspired by God, without maintaining that Genesis is intended to give a scientific account of the way in which the world began. We must not judge it as though this was the intention. *But it is true.* It teaches vitally important truths about God, about mankind, and about the world in which we live.

Such literature is every bit as important as a scientific essay on the origins of the universe.

Who first collected these books together to form the Bible? And why did they choose *these* books, and omit others?

When they wrote, the authors were not aware that they were writing 'holy scripture'. Some described periods of Israelite history. Others recorded important laws. Some told stories. A few wrote down sermons preached by prophets or apostles. Others gave advice.

They didn't think to themselves, 'Now I am writing a part of the Bible'. But as they wrote they were inspired and guided by God. Their work has unique importance. But this doesn't mean that they were just human typewriters, writing with their eyes shut! Their writing style, their personalities and their lives were used by God to express his message for the world.

But why these books?

How did these particular books come to be collected together to form the Bible? The broad answer is:
● over a long period of time;
● after a great deal of prayer, discussion — and argument!

The Old Testament

During the centuries before Jesus, the Jews had begun to think of various writings as Scripture. Above all, they valued the first five books in our Old Testament — 'the Torah' or 'Law'. Another name is 'the Pentateuch' ('Pent' means five).

Many Jews also placed great importance on 'the Prophets'. This group of scrolls included most of the sixteen books which carry the name of a prophet in our Bible (Daniel was placed elsewhere). It also included some books of history — Joshua, Judges, Samuel and Kings. These books show God at work in the life of the nation.

The third group of scrolls they called 'the Writings'. This group includes Job, Proverbs and Psalms.

The Jews came to believe that these three groups of scrolls were worthy to be read in the synagogue as God's word. Some differences of opinion existed concerning the position or worthiness of a few scrolls. In AD 90 a council of Jewish teachers (Rabbis) met at Jamnia in Israel to resolve these problems. Today's Hebrew Bible contains the books accepted at that council.

The Bible is taught and discussed in many different parts of the world. Its stories and teaching are about real life, and about how God fits into the picture.

The New Testament

Shortly after the death and resurrection of Jesus, groups of Christians met for prayer, fellowship and worship. They read the Jewish scriptures together. In addition, the teaching of Jesus was read aloud, together with letters from John, Peter, Paul and other Christian leaders.

As the years passed, a large number of Christian letters and books were written. Some of these came to be honoured as 'holy scripture', but there was no complete agreement. So in time it became necessary to decide exactly which Christian books should count as holy Scripture, alongside the Jewish scriptures. This question was discussed at length. The final decision was reached by church leaders in the fourth century.

God speaks

Christians believe that this process of discussion shows how God speaks to us. He could have sent a ready-made Bible from heaven. Instead, he chose to work through human authors — guiding them and helping them, but not by-passing them.

The same principle applies as Christians *read* the Bible. It does not give simple, clear answers to all our problems and decisions. Instead, it gives principles which we need to apply after hard thought, discussion and prayer. But some Bible teaching is very clear indeed — especially when it tells us about:

● God's love for the world which he made;

● God's involvement in the world: by his Son and by his Spirit;

● God's invitation to trust in him;

● God's instructions to us; to love, to forgive, and to pray.

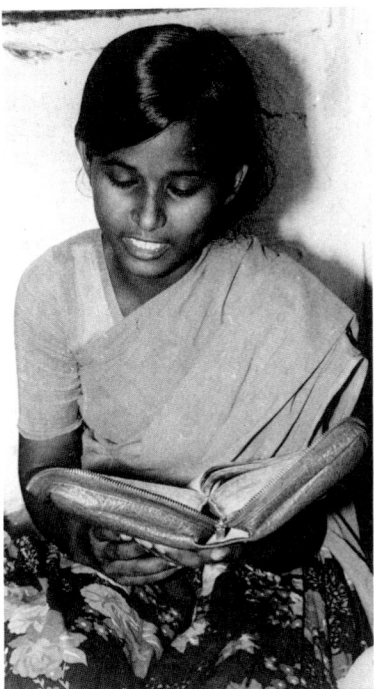

Christians often read the Bible to help them make decisions about the way they live.

Astronauts read the Bible

Christmas Day 1968 was a great day in the history of space research. The American Apollo 8 team circled the moon, and they spoke by radio to many nations. The words they decided to broadcast to the world were the opening verses of the Bible:

'In the beginning, God created the heavens and the earth . . .'

Problems

Read the Bible carefully, and you run into problems. One problem concerns Genesis — the very first book. Can we really believe in Adam and Eve? And if we do, can we still believe in the scientific explanation of the beginning of the world?

Another problem concerns the violence which is recorded – especially in the Old Testament.

Violence

The Bible – especially the Old Testament – is a very violent book. Battles are common, and the Israelites often prayed for God's help as they fought.

From the beginning God taught his people that they must exercise justice and care – even to visitors from other countries. But the ancient world was a violent world. Fighting between nations was universal, and the Israelites were no exception.

Slowly, over the centuries, God taught them more about love and forgiveness. The climax came when Jesus told his astonished hearers: 'Love your enemies.'

He put his own teaching into practice. On the cross he prayed for the men who drove nails through his hands and feet: 'Forgive them, Father! They don't know what they are doing.'

In August each year, thousands of young people in Britain gather for a rock music festival called Greenbelt. This is a festival with a difference. Music, music, music . . . and the Bible. A whole variety of meetings are held over the weekend, to study different aspects of the teaching of the Bible.

The attendance is about 25,000 and most pop festivals of this size need a large number of police to keep order. In 1983 the official police 'force' at Greenbelt was halved: from 4 to 2!

The Old Testament begins with a bold claim: 'In the beginning God created the heavens and the earth.' It goes on to describe the way in which men and women disobeyed God — bringing conflict and sin into the world.

The rest of the Bible shows how God set out to rescue the human race from its own sinfulness and selfishness. God chose to concentrate on one small nation — and to use these people to speak to the whole world.

That nation was ancient Israel, and the Old Testament is the story of the Israelites. It describes their early life as slaves in Egypt and their wonderful escape, called the Exodus. It tells of their wanderings and their rise to power. It charts their problems, their triumphs and their joys.

And it shows how God gradually taught them about himself — what he is like, and what he required of them. He did this by giving them laws, leaders and teachers.

Great laws

In particular he gave them Ten Commandments. These remain at the root of the law-codes in every country in the western world today.

Many of the more detailed laws are concerned with worship and with justice. God required the Israelites to take special care of powerless people – especially visitors, orphans and widows.

Great leaders

● **Abraham** — the father of the nation, whose faith in God was strong and firm. God gave him a command; 'Get up and go!' So he did. With his family, his servants and his animals, he travelled from Ur to Canaan. The New Testament looks back to Abraham's active

One Sabbath (Saturday) I was invited to worship in a Jewish synagogue. As I went in I was greeted warmly and given a small cap to wear on my head.

In the Service there was a great deal of singing and reading. Almost all the words — whether read or sung — came from the Jewish scriptures. At one point, large scrolls of scripture were carried joyfully in procession around the synagogue by young men.

This was a powerful reminder that Jews and Christians have a great deal in common. For the entire Jewish scriptures are contained within the Christian Bible, where they are called the Old Testament.

The Old Testament was written from right to left in ancient Hebrew. Although it is ancient, the Old Testament can still speak directly to modern societies.

faith as a turning point in human history. He is the 'father' of all who trust in God.

● **Moses** — who led the people from slavery in Egypt. Before they entered the 'promised land' of Canaan, Moses led them through difficult years of hardship in the wilderness. These hardships taught the people to trust in God and to obey his laws.

● **David** — Israel's greatest king. David was a man of action. He was also skilled as a musician and as a poet. But he had many faults. The Bible describes these very honestly. It never whitewashes its heroes: it shows them as they are. Despite this, God gave David a great promise. This was fulfilled when Jesus was born a thousand years later. Jesus was a descendant of David — and an even greater king.

The Bible's first five books are called 'the Torah', or 'the Law'. They are fundamental to both Judaism and Christianity.

Great prophets

Several Old Testament books carry the names of prophets. Isaiah, Jeremiah, Ezekiel, Micah, Hosea and Amos are some of these. The prophets continually called the people back to God. They encouraged their hearers to trust God in times of difficulty, to welcome strangers, and to help the poor. When national leaders went astray and ignored justice for ordinary people, the prophets spoke out against them — and often found themselves in trouble.

Great poets

The Israelites did not develop their abilities as artists and sculptors. The second of the Ten Commandments tells us why. In the ancient world, men and women were tempted to worship pictures or sculptures as idols. So God forbade them to create works of art containing men, women or animals, because they might worship them as gods.

Instead they concentrated their artistic talents on buildings and words — especially on words.

Many of the prophets were fine poets. And each of the 150 Psalms in the Old Testament is a Hebrew poem.

The language of the Old Testament

Go to Israel today and you will hear modern Hebrew. In 1948 the modern State of Israel was founded. Jews came from many different countries to settle there, and they spoke many different languages. The Hebrew language was 're-invented' to meet this situation.

Hebrew was spoken in Israel in Old Testament times — and the Jewish scriptures (the Christian Old Testament) were originally written in that language. But by the time of Jesus, two important changes had taken place:
● **The Hebrew language** had been replaced by Aramaic in Israel. However, the scriptures continued to be read in Hebrew in synagogue services because it was regarded as a holy language.
● **The Greek language** had come to hold the position of English in the modern world. It was the international language — spoken in more countries than any other tongue.

Because many Jews in Jesus' time had settled in countries outside Israel, they understood Greek better than Hebrew or Aramaic. So, for their benefit, the Hebrew scriptures were translated into Greek. This important translation is called the Septuagint, because seventy translators were said to have worked on it.

Hebrew is written from right to left. So you open a Hebrew Bible at the back — rather as you read a news-paper if you look at the sports reports first!

Greek is written from left to right, like other European languages.

A Book which strengthens

Sir Geoffrey Jackson was British Ambassador in Uruguay. In January 1971 he was captured by terrorists. For several months he experienced terrible conditions — he was kept in a tiny cell, and he knew that at any moment he might be killed.

His Christian faith was a tremendous help as he fought to keep calm and sane. Eventually he was given books, and a bed. Two books were particularly important to him. One was Leo Tolstoy's great novel — *Anna Karenina*. The other was a Bible — first in Spanish, then in English.

Scientists read The Bible

In Britain, the Research Scientists Christian Fellowship has several hundred members. These scientists study the Bible regularly — in groups and on their own. They see no conflict between their faith in God, and their scientific activities.

America and Eastern Europe

In America, 1983 was called 'the Year of the Bible'. The United States Congress said that this was in recognition 'of both the formative influence the Bible has been for our nation, and our national need to study and apply the teachings of the Holy Scriptures.' In contrast, Bibles are in short supply in some Eastern European countries. But import licences are granted by some governments, and Bibles are sometimes printed on the official communist presses.

A typical year

About 10 million complete Bibles, 12 million New Testaments, 30 million single books and 400 million scripture leaflets were distributed around the world in 1981.

FROM THE PAST

The Bible gives a detailed picture of life in the ancient world. Modern archaeology has unearthed objects that show the Bible's picture to be remarkably accurate. **Below** A legal document from 1750 BC. It is written in cuneiform on a clay tablet and has its own clay 'envelope'.

Right Probably the oldest map in the world, dating from 2300 BC. It shows the world as a circle surrounded by the 'Salt Sea'. Babylon is at its centre.

Below This carving shows the Assyrian Emperor, Ashurbanipal, killing a lion. The Assyrians took many of the Jewish people into exile during Bible times.

Left A head-dress from the royal tombs at Ur. The flowers and leaves were cut from sheets of gold.

Below A beaten gold bowl from the famous Oxus Treasure. The treasure was part of the riches of the Persian Empire, described in the Bible.

Below An Egyptian model found in a tomb shows how bread was made in ancient times. One of the figures can be clearly seen kneading the dough.

5.5 PROPHETS OF AN AGE TO COME

It was wartime. The allies were expecting a very important Visitor. He had vital information which could win the war.

Preparations for his visit were very thorough. Thousands of words had been written to ensure that key people were accurately informed. But no one knew *when* he would arrive.

One day a General wrote a letter giving up-to-date information. As he completed his letter, the Visitor arrived. The General had often dreamt of this moment but, at first, he was disappointed. The Visitor seemed rather ordinary.

But as they talked the General was inspired and convinced. *This* was the man. Before sending his letter he added a postscript. It read: 'The time has come. He has arrived. Everything looks different now.'

Jesus often told stories with an underlying meaning. These 'parables' were about everyday events — a wedding; a woman who lost a coin. Sometimes they were very dramatic — about a man who was mugged or a son who returned home after a long time away. This war story is modelled on Jesus' parables. It is intended to explain the relationship between the Old and the New Testament.

The Old Testament is rather like the General's letter. It is important in its own right and for its own sake. The letter contained important information about troop movements. The Old Testament contains important information — about right and wrong, about justice, about God.

But — like the letter — the Old Testament looks forward. It is full of expectation, full of hope, full of

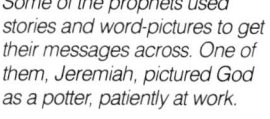

Some of the prophets used stories and word-pictures to get their messages across. One of them, Jeremiah, pictured God as a potter, patiently at work.

promise. The General expected a great Visitor who would transform the situation. So did the Jews. They called him the Messiah or the Christ.

Promises

In particular, it was the prophets of the Old Testament who looked forward. They weren't mere fortune-tellers — they were very concerned with their own times. Their chief task was to call their own people back to the ways of God.

But God gave to the prophets a wonderful gift of insight. And he gave them marvellous promises to pass on to their people. These promises had many strands.

● **Isaiah** spoke about a baby who would grow up to be an even greater ruler than King David. He would be called by many great names such as 'Wonderful Counsellor', 'Mighty God' and 'Prince of Peace'.

● **Jeremiah** spoke about a future new age. This age would be marked by a new covenant. Men and women would know God; God's law would be in their hearts; their sins would be forgiven.

● **Ezekiel** had a vision in which he saw a valley full of dry bones. God's word brought the bones back to life. It was a great promise to Israel. The prophet encouraged them to renew their trust in God. He knew that God gives life, and can transform every situation.

● **Daniel** described a great king who would rule for all eternity. This eternal king was 'like a Son of Man'. When Jesus came he taught about the kingdom of God. And he often referred to himself as 'the Son of Man'.

● **Isaiah** described God's suffering servant. These 'Servant passages' are perhaps the most remarkable

prophecies of all. Isaiah spoke first of the nation; then of just one person who would suffer for his people. Reading chapter 53 of Isaiah's prophecy is like reading a description of the death of Jesus — even though this took place hundreds of years later.

This is not to say that the prophets had crystal clear ideas about Jesus. They spoke about events and people in their own times: but, under God's guidance, their words had a deeper meaning. Hundreds of years later the early Christians read the prophets' words. They realised that the prophecies had been fulfilled at a deeper level: fulfilled in Jesus, whose name means 'God saves'.

This street preacher in New York brings the Bible's message to life for today. The prophets of the Old Testament did the same for people in their times.

Digging for past civilizations

Over the past 100 years, archaeologists have been very active. They have dug and examined many places mentioned in the Bible. All this activity has done three things:

● **It has shed a great deal of light on the Bible.** We now understand the customs, the attitudes and the history of Bible people much more clearly.

● **It has caused some puzzles**, for some points of Bible history and geography don't easily 'fit'.

● **It has backed up the basic historical reliability of the Bible:** 'It is a fact that, by and large, modern archaeological science has done a great deal to confirm the accuracy of the history recorded in the Bible, and only rarely and in relatively unimportant matters does it put a question mark against the biblical record' (Professor I H Marshall of the University of Aberdeen).

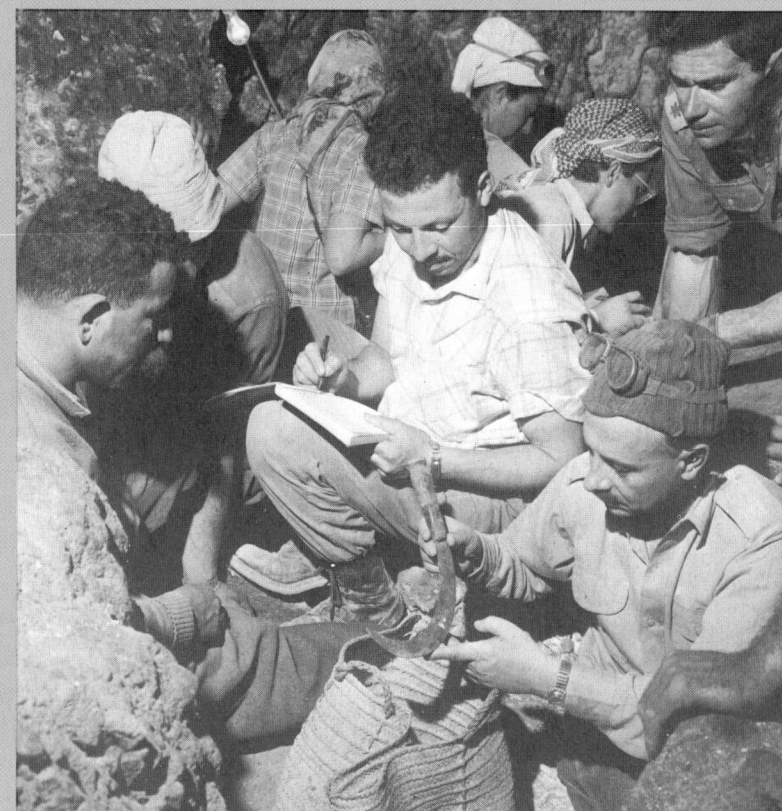

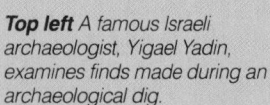

Top left A famous Israeli archaeologist, Yigael Yadin, examines finds made during an archaeological dig.

Opposite page Excavating the temple wall in Jerusalem. These enormous stones were laid in the time of Herod the Great, a few years before Jesus was born.

Human remains have also helped in rediscovering what life was like in ancient times.

5.6 FOUR BOOKS WITH ONE MESSAGE

THISISNOTASEASY-TOREADASIT-MIGHTBEWHY

In the early Greek New Testament manuscripts sentences were not punctuated, and words were not separated. This can cause problems. Some phrases can have at least two possible — and very different — meanings. Try this one (which isn't in the Bible) and see!

GODISNOWHERE

In fact, experts are very skilled in reading the manuscripts. Despite the problems, we can be sure that we have a reliable translation of the Bible.

The key days in all history

It has been suggested that the birth, death and resurrection of Jesus and the day of Pentecost are the four key days in all history. Why?

The Jewish scriptures consist only of what Christians call the Old Testament. Christians see the Old Testament as a preparation for the coming of Jesus — for the *New* Testament.

The New Testament begins with four accounts of the life and ministry of Jesus. These accounts are called Gospels. They are remarkable in four ways:

● **Remarkable literature.** The Gospels are unique. Nothing like them had ever been written before. Once they were in circulation, other authors tried to imitate them, but without success. Christians believe these short documents to be the most important books in the entire world, for they speak of the most important person. Through these ancient documents, each new generation can hear the voice of Jesus. His words are fresh and relevant in every age.

● **Remarkable omissions!** The Gospels leave out some surprising material. We read quite a lot about the birth of Jesus, and Luke describes one incident when Jesus was twelve years old. Apart from this we know next to nothing about his boyhood, his teenage years, or his work as a village carpenter in Nazareth.

Was Jesus tall? Did he have a beard? What colour were his eyes? Was he good looking? Many painters and film directors have tried to answer these questions — but it is guesswork. The men who wrote the Gospels give us very few clues.

● **Remarkable content.** Instead, the Gospels are concerned almost entirely with the teaching and ministry of Jesus — and with his death. After the accounts of his birth by Luke and Matthew we are thrust forward about thirty years.

The four Gospels tell us about a real, historical person — Jesus, the carpenter from Nazareth.

We learn that Jesus left home, called his twelve disciples, and travelled around his country on foot, teaching and performing miracles.

● **Remarkable ending.** In most biographies, it is the *life* of the central figure which is of central importance. The death of the person is described, but it isn't usually given all that much space. The Gospels are different. For example, one-third of Mark's short Gospel describes the last few days of Jesus' life. Other writers in the New Testament lay a similar emphasis on the death of Jesus. The writers are convinced that the day on which Jesus died is one of the most important days in all history.

But the Gospels do not end with the death of Jesus. They end with his resurrection — his rising from death. Sometimes the disciples to whom he appeared didn't immediately recognize him. Some refused to believe. But the evidence was too strong. It really *was* him. He proved it to them by talking with them and by eating with them. He even invited one disciple — doubting Thomas — to touch him.

You are alive today because of an event in the past — your birth. Christians believe that Jesus is alive today because of an event in the past — his resurrection. His final great promise, recorded in Matthew's Gospel, is: 'I will be with you always, to the end of the age'.

In the New Testament the meaning of the death of Jesus is illustrated in many ways. It is described as:
● a sacrifice for sins
● a great battle between God and evil
● a man dying for his enemies
● a shepherd giving his life to protect his sheep
● a ransom paid to free slaves from captivity
● the fulfilment of Old Testament prophecies
● a wonderful example of selfless love.

See section 3 **The Easter Faith** to follow up these ideas.

This legal document is in Aramaic. It was written using pen and ink on clay, and was found in Egypt.

The language of the New Testament

If you travelled back in time to hear Jesus teaching in Jerusalem, you would hear several languages. Jesus probably spoke at least two of these:
● **Aramaic** was used by those who lived in Judea where Jesus was born and where he died. It was also spoken in Galilee where Jesus was brought up.
● **Greek** was readily understood in most Mediterranean countries. This meant that people from different nations could speak freely to one another. After the resurrection of Jesus this common language allowed his followers to spread the good news quickly to many countries.

The New Testament is written in Greek. But in Mark's Gospel we find a few of the Aramaic words used by Jesus.

The Gospels may be remarkable — but are they true? The Evangelists (as Matthew, Mark, Luke and John are called) believed Jesus to be the Messiah. They are not unbiased reporters. They wanted to convince their readers about Jesus.

Not all of them were first-hand reporters, either, and none of the four Gospels is actually signed by its author. Careful detective work is needed to find out who wrote what.

The names Matthew, Mark, Luke and John were attached to the Gospels *after* they were written. Matthew's Gospel *may* have been written by Matthew the tax-collector, and John's Gospel *may* have been written by John the son of Zebedee. If so, they were disciples of Jesus who knew him very well. Mark probably saw Jesus but he wasn't one of the original twelve disciples. Luke certainly didn't know Jesus personally: he makes this clear.

But, despite these problems, we can be confident of the reliability of the Gospels. Consider these facts about the authors.

● **They wrote about Jesus, who stressed honesty.** A central theme of his teaching is 'the kingdom of God'. Jesus made it clear that people who accept God's rule in their lives should be open and honest. It is very difficult to believe that the Gospel writers would use lies to spread a message about truth.

● **They could be contradicted.** Jesus died about AD 30. The four Gospels were probably completed between AD 60 and AD 90. But most of the information in the Gospels was in circulation much earlier than this. It was heard and read by people who had been in the crowds that followed Jesus. If someone had distorted or invented information about Jesus his hearers

At a press conference, each writer or photographer records his or her own angle on a story. The Gospel writers give us four different angles on Jesus.

The 'Evangelists'

The four Gospels are named after Matthew, Mark, Luke and John. These four men are called 'Evangelists' because the Gospels describe the good news of God's love for the world shown through Jesus. The word gospel means 'good news'. So does the Greek word *evangel*.

Modern preachers are sometimes called 'evangelists' because they bring people this same good news.

would have been quick to contradict. We have a record of some of the rumours circulated to discredit the early Christians. But we have no evidence which seriously questions the Gospel accounts.

● **They did a lot of travelling, listening and studying.** Jesus made a tremendous impact on those who heard and saw him. People would rush home and tell their families and friends about him. A good deal of his teaching was in the form of poetry and parable. It was easy to remember — and Eastern memories were (and are) good!

Writing was quite common, too. Jesus' words were repeated in sermons and conversations. Some of these were written down on scraps of 'papyrus' (a type of paper) and eventually on scrolls. So Jesus' teaching was circulated among groups of believers at an early date. All this happened before the Gospels were completed — and this spoken and written material was used by the Evangelists.

Luke, in particular, makes it very clear that he sifted a lot of evidence before writing his Gospel. He was a doctor — well-educated and sensitive. He travelled a great deal, often with the apostle Paul. He talked to many people and read other documents before writing his Gospel. He was very concerned to convince his readers, and he knew that accuracy was extremely important.

● **They met people who knew Jesus, or saw him themselves.** Mark was probably the first Evangelist to complete his Gospel. It is very likely that he had seen Jesus. He records an amusing episode in his account of the trial of Jesus (see Mark 14:51-52). The young man was probably Mark himself.

But — more important — Mark

was a friend of Peter. An early historian called Papias tells us that Mark wrote down what Peter preached. And no one knew Jesus better than Peter.

Concerning Matthew's Gospel and John's Gospel there are various possibilities. Perhaps they were written by the Matthew and John who were members of the original twelve disciples. Perhaps these Gospels were written by authors who acted as editors or secretaries for the original Matthew and John. We cannot be sure.

The word 'perhaps' is significant. The Gospels have been more closely studied by brilliant minds than any other documents. This is a wonderful tribute to their power and importance. All this work has yielded a great deal of insight and understanding. But the experts still disagree about many details. And many fascinating questions remain unanswered because they don't have enough background information.

● **They wrote down many hard things.** Many episodes in the Gospels show the apostles in a bad light: slow to understand, greedy for power and position, not very heroic. This is remarkable, for the Gospels were written to feed the faith of the early church — and the apostles were the leaders of that church. We might have expected them to cover up these details. The fact that they didn't points to the reliability of the Gospels. They told the story of Jesus, and of his followers, *as it really was.*

● **They left out some convenient themes.** The early Christians faced many problems and had many difficult decisions to take. For example, when non-Jews (Gentiles) were converted to Christ, did they need to keep all the details of the Jewish Law? It was a great problem. In fact, it nearly split the church in two.

This problem could have been solved very easily if Jesus had given an answer. But he didn't. The Gospel writers could have invented some instructions and said that these were the words of Jesus. This would have saved a great deal of anguish and argument. The fact that they did not do so is another pointer towards their honesty.

● **They wrote.** An obvious thing to say — but very important all the same. When Jesus died, his disciples were shattered. They were frightened and depressed. They thought it was all over.

But very soon they were full of confidence and joy. They launched the biggest, most influential movement which the world has ever seen — and the written Gospels were part of that movement.

The great energy and joy of the first Christians came from their certainty that God had raised Jesus from the dead. Accounts of the appearances of Jesus after his death are included in the Gospels. Without these appearances the disciples would have remained very disappointed. The Gospels would never have been written, and the world would never have heard of Jesus.

● **The four Gospels are different.** If you talk to four people who saw a dramatic event — a fire or an accident, for example — two things become clear. First: *truthful witnesses tell different stories.* Different aspects of any event stand out for different individuals. They describe the event from a personal angle. Second: *truthful witnesses tell the same story.* Despite the differences, you can easily recognize that they are describing the same event.

The Gospels are like this. They include different material and they emphasize different points. But they tell the same basic story.

The differences between the Gospels show their genuineness. This was no conspiracy. We have four honest men, each giving his own version of the good news. Despite their different emphases, they tell the same basic story. And the same towering figure shines through. They passionately believe that Jesus, who taught and healed in first-century Palestine, is the Son of God — the light and Saviour of the world.

Four books

● **Mark's Gospel** is brief and full of action. We are taken from place to place at high speed. He stops occasionally to recount the teaching of Jesus, but he concentrates on his travels and miracles.

● **Matthew's Gospel** is organized round five blocks of Jesus' teaching. Matthew's Jewish background is clear, but he includes the story of the wise men from the East who visited the infant Jesus. In this way, Matthew makes it clear that *all* the nations are invited to worship the Christ.

● **Luke's Gospel** is the only one by a non-Jewish writer. He highlights Jesus' concern for outcasts and second-class citizens — prostitutes, beggars and tax collectors. He includes the parable of the prodigal son — a powerful reminder that God's love and forgiveness are available to everyone. He was concerned to get down the facts about Jesus for the whole non-Jewish world.

● **John's Gospel** was almost certainly written later than the others. It includes events not recorded by the other Gospel writers, and is the result of deep reflection on the significance of Jesus. Key material for understanding the teaching and mission of Jesus is collected under a series of 'signs'. Because the Gospel of John stands apart, Matthew, Mark and Luke are sometimes grouped together and called 'the Synoptic Gospels' ('synoptic' means 'with one viewpoint').

5.8 LUKE, PETER AND PAUL

Luke

Luke wrote over one quarter of the New Testament — more than any other author. He wrote the Acts of the Apostles as the sequel to his Gospel.

The book of Acts describes the early days of the Christian church. It opens with a small group of disciples waiting in Jerusalem, as Jesus had instructed. This was just before his ascension into heaven.

On a Jewish festival called Pentecost, God's Spirit came upon them in great power. After that it was all action. The good news of Jesus spread at high speed through the various countries around the Mediterranean Sea.

Of all the men and women described in Acts, two stand out: Peter and Paul.·

Peter

Peter was one of the original twelve disciples of Jesus. From the Gospels we learn that he was fiery and impetuous. He often made mistakes, and when Jesus was on trial for his life, Peter lost his nerve. When a servant girl challenged him, he swore and denied all knowledge of Jesus.

Later, Peter wept with shame and found it hard to forgive himself. But Jesus forgave him — and gave him the responsibility of leadership in the early church. His main work was inspiring and encouraging his fellow believers, and convincing his fellow Jews that Jesus was the Messiah.

Paul

At this time Paul (known then by his Jewish name, Saul) was a rigid Jew. He was a member of the party of the Pharisees, and he believed that the Christians were God's enemies. So he supported the execution 'by stoning' of a Christian preacher called Stephen in about AD 35. Stephen died with great courage, and as he died he prayed — asking Jesus to forgive his executioners. Stephen's deep faith made a great impact on Paul.

But he continued to persecute the Christians. He travelled as far as Syria to hunt them down. It was as he approached Damascus — the capital of Syria — that Jesus appeared to him.

In the Book of Acts, Paul described what happened. He saw a brilliant light which blinded him. Then he heard the voice of Jesus. Paul became convinced that Stephen had been right all along. He was baptized and restored to health. From that moment he used his tremendous energy and ability to tell other people about Jesus.

Paul's message

Paul told people about:
- **Jesus the Messiah**, who had fulfilled the Jewish scriptures.
- **Jesus' death** on the cross and his resurrection to new life.
- **God's love** — shown in creation, and in sending his Son.
- **God's power** — shown by raising Jesus from the dead.
- **God's free gifts** — forgiveness and eternal life cannot be earned by religious acts and moral deeds. They can only be received by faith in Jesus, and by turning from sin.

Travels

Luke describes Paul's many travels. He was in a good position to do so, for they were friends and often travelled together. Paul's life was action-packed — riots and shipwreck; crowds and hostility; friends and encouragement; arrest and prison; snakes and earthquakes; beatings and escapes.

As he travelled, Paul preached to anyone who would listen, whether Jew or Gentile. Paul's preaching often caused noisy opposition. But always there were some who were pleased to hear him. Churches were formed in the places where he preached. These churches contained slaves and other 'unimportant' people. They often met in people's homes. Later they met secretly in places such as the catacombs in Rome, to avoid persecution.

Other preachers and teachers were at work, too. A church was founded in Rome itself — the capital of the mighty Roman Empire.

In the time of Paul, the Romans had swept pirates off the seas, making travel much safer. Paul used ships, like this corn-carrying ship, many times in his travels.

Letters

Paul and Peter were great pastors. They were very concerned that the small Christian communities should stand firm despite the temptations and pressures which surrounded them. So they wrote letters, giving advice and encouragement — and even rebuke.

About one third of the New Testament is made up of letters. Thirteen of these are signed by Paul, and two by Peter. John wrote three, James one, Jude one, and one letter is anonymous. These letters spell out principles for living the Christian life which apply in every age. Nearly two thousand years later, Christians read these letters, not as interesting curios from the past, but to hear God's living voice today.

The book of Acts ends with Paul under house-arrest in Rome. There is a strong tradition that he and Peter were killed there in the terrible persecution against Christians in AD 64. The Emperor Nero needed a scapegoat for the fire which swept through Rome, and he blamed the Christians. Peter was crucified, but he said he was not worthy to die like Jesus. So he was crucified upside down.

This time, his courage did not fail.

The New Testament letters were probably written using pens very like these. They date from Roman times and are made of reed. The pen case still contains black ink, centuries after it dried up.

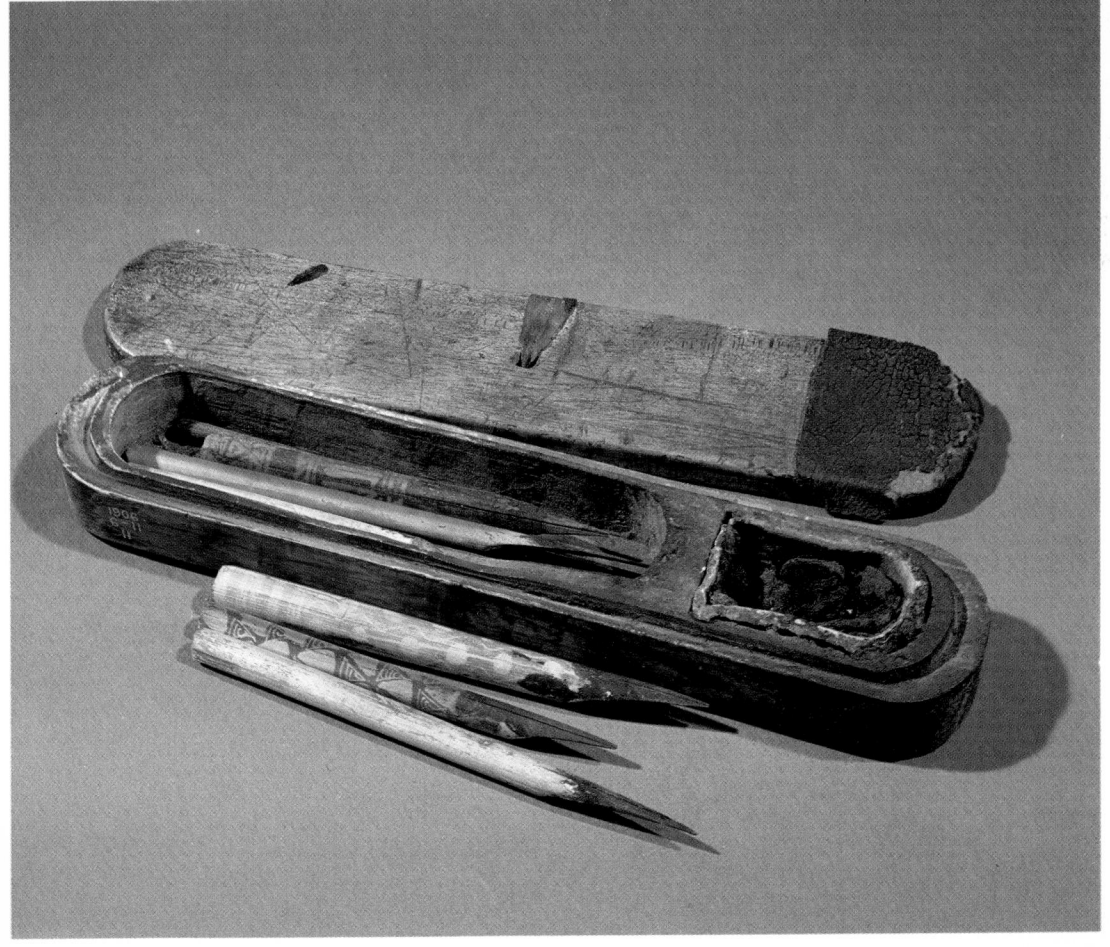

Translation headaches!

The following examples from the Bible Society show some of the problems faced by Bible translators:

● A translator belonging to the Turkana people in Northern Kenya sent a report in his own language which said 'The translation is going down hill fast.' Translated into English this means things are going very well. After all, going down hill is less exhausting than going up hill!

● In the Malagasy language there is no word for hypocrite. The translation reads 'like a woman who puts a new raffia mat on an unswept floor'. Obviously a translation thought out by a man!

There are at least 5,000 languages spoken in the world. About 3,000 of these languages do not have even one book of the Bible. By the end of 1982 only 279 of them had a complete Bible. By 1992 the Bible Societies aim to increase that number so that every official language, and every language with a million speakers, will have a complete Bible.

The shoemaker

William Carey was an English shoemaker, and had little formal education. But he was a brilliant linguist and a pioneer of the modern missionary movement. He sailed to India in 1793 and translated the Bible (sometimes complete, often in smaller sections) into 25 different languages and dialects.

Mary Jones grew up in Wales at the end of the 18th century. She loved to see and touch the big family Bible in a friend's home. When she was ten, she went to school (it was optional then!) because she wanted to read the Bible for herself.

Mary longed to have her own Bible. She did odd jobs so that she could buy one. When she was sixteen, she walked 26 miles in her bare feet, to buy a copy. But the Bibles had been sold.

She was so upset that Thomas Charles, a Christian minister, found her a copy. Thomas was very impressed by Mary's attitude and he told the Religious Tract Society in London. As a result, the British and Foreign Bible Society was founded in 1804.

The movement spread, and today there are about one hundred Bible Societies spread throughout the world. The aim remains the same: to provide a Bible for every person who wants to read it.

Worldwide

Over the centuries many people have been so gripped by the message of the Bible that they have wanted to see it brought to others — in their own language, or in other languages worldwide:

● At the time of the rediscovery of the great ancient languages and the invention of printing in the 15th century, the Bible was translated into European languages such as English and German. Printing brought the Bible to ordinary people.

● Missionaries, from the 16th century on, went with the explorers

to the newly-discovered lands.
● In the 19th century, Bible Societies were formed to translate and distribute Bibles in many different languages.
● In the 20th century, many new English translations and other modern translations have been produced worldwide. Specialist agencies such as Wycliffe Bible Translators have translated the Bible into tribal languages. Bibles have been distributed worldwide as never before — but much work remains to be done.

Left *Translating the Bible is not easy — after all, it is a large book! Christians who translate the Bible do so because they want to reach people who have never heard its message.*

The biggest-ever airlift of Bibles

In 1982 there was a great shortage of Bibles in Uganda. To meet the demand, a load of Bibles weighing 69 tons was sent. The load went from England to Holland by ship; from Holland to Germany by road; from Germany to Uganda by air.

The load filled two 707 jets. The Bibles — 100,000 of them — were in English and Lugaunda. Two days after leaving Frankfurt, the Bibles were on sale in Kampala.

At present the Bible Societies are involved in scripture translation projects in 574 different languages around the world. In 375 of these projects some part of the Bible is being translated for the very first time.

Wanted! 1,000 million Bibles

In China, during the Communist 'Cultural Revolution' of the 1960s, Christian activity was very limited. But churches have not only survived but sprung up and grown. In October 1980 the New Testament in Chinese was reprinted. By the end of the same year, the entire Bible was published. More people speak Chinese than any other language. English is spoken in more countries throughout the world than any other tongue.

A massive consignment of Chinese Bibles wait to be shipped.

Through the ages Christians believe that God has spoken to people in many different ways: through dreams, visions and voices; through sermons and prophets; through circumstances or ordinary conversations.

Some occasions are reported to have been very dramatic. At twenty-one, Dorothy Kerin was dying from tuberculosis. One night she was so ill that her doctor thought she would die. Her pulse appeared to stop for eight minutes. Then Dorothy spoke to someone whom no one else could see. She ate a meal (cold beef and pickled walnuts!), slept, and recovered.

Dorothy claims that she saw Jesus, and that he spoke to her. She lived for fifty more very active years and had a very remarkable healing ministry.

Listening to God

Few experience such dramatic events. But Christians believe that each of us can hear God's voice through the Bible.

There are two basic requirements:
● We need a Bible in our own language.
● We need to read that Bible with a 'listening' attitude.

God can speak to us through any part of the Bible — even the most 'difficult' parts of the Old Testament. Christians believe that the voice of God is heard at its clearest in the New Testament —

One page is better than nothing

A few villagers brought three Bibles back to share with their families and neighbours in Long Nowong, Indonesia. Each day the villagers got together to listen as it was read.

The number of people who believed and accepted the good news of Jesus Christ grew steadily. The result was a mass baptism of 1,123 people.

They each wanted the Scriptures so much that they decided to split up the three Bibles they had: that way each of them could have at least one page!

and especially in the Gospels. The writer of the Letter to the Hebrews in the New Testament sums up the Christian viewpoint:

'In the past, God spoke to our ancestors many times and in many ways through the prophets, but in these last days he has spoken to us through his Son.'
Hebrews 1:1

A life saving book

The Masai people in Kenya built a dam. In 1976 it burst, and all their precious water was lost. Rice powder was flown in to prevent starvation. According to Masai custom, old people are given food; young people must find their own. An evangelist explained the teaching of the Bible — God loves *everyone*, old and young alike. The elders considered this, and agreed that the food should be shared with the young people too.

The Gospels

'The gospels are not biographies and do not pretend to be. They are more like portraits and they differ just as four portraits of the same person would differ.'
Trevor Shannon

St. Mark's Gospel: 'the most important document in the history of the world.'
Stuart Blanch

Christians do not read the Bible out of a sense of duty. They do it because they expect to hear God speaking through it to them.

'It is not the parts of Scripture that I don't understand that worry me, it is the parts that I do understand!'
Mark Twain

The map

That is how Christians see the Bible.
● It is not merely superb literature.
● It is not merely a source book for Christian beliefs.
● It is not a lucky dip where any verse can be squeezed to fit any situation.
The Bible is a map.
● It is a guide for the Christian community as they travel through this life.
● It is a library, full of poetry, history, letters and the like.
● It is designed by God to give us enough information to live a joyful, useful, upright and loving life in this world. It is a map, with guidelines, warnings, examples, teaching, encouragement.
Michael Green

5.11 THE BIBLE'S FOCUS

'So Jesus came to Nazareth, where he had been brought up, and went to synagogue on the Sabbath day as he regularly did. He stood up to read the lesson and was handed the scroll of the prophet Isaiah. He opened the scroll and found the passage which says,
"The spirit of the Lord is upon me because he has anointed me; he has sent me to announce good news to the poor, to proclaim release for prisoners and recovery of sight for the blind; to let the broken victims go free, to proclaim the year of the Lord's favour."
He rolled up the scroll, gave it back to the attendant, and sat down; and all eyes in the synagogue were fixed on him.
He began to speak: "Today", he said, "in your very hearing this text has come true."'
Luke 4:16-21

Right through this section on the Bible, we have seen that Jesus is the focus of the whole Bible.

The Old Testament leads up to him: the world, created by God to be so good, has gone wrong. Despite God's law and his love for his people, only a completely fresh start will make it possible for people to live in harmony with God.

Jesus came as that new start. The New Testament tells us about him. He lived a perfect life, taught a new creation, died to make it possible, rose again as the first citizen of the new kingdom. The New Testament letters explore all that this means for his people, the church.

The Bible is more than just a book to read. It changes lives.

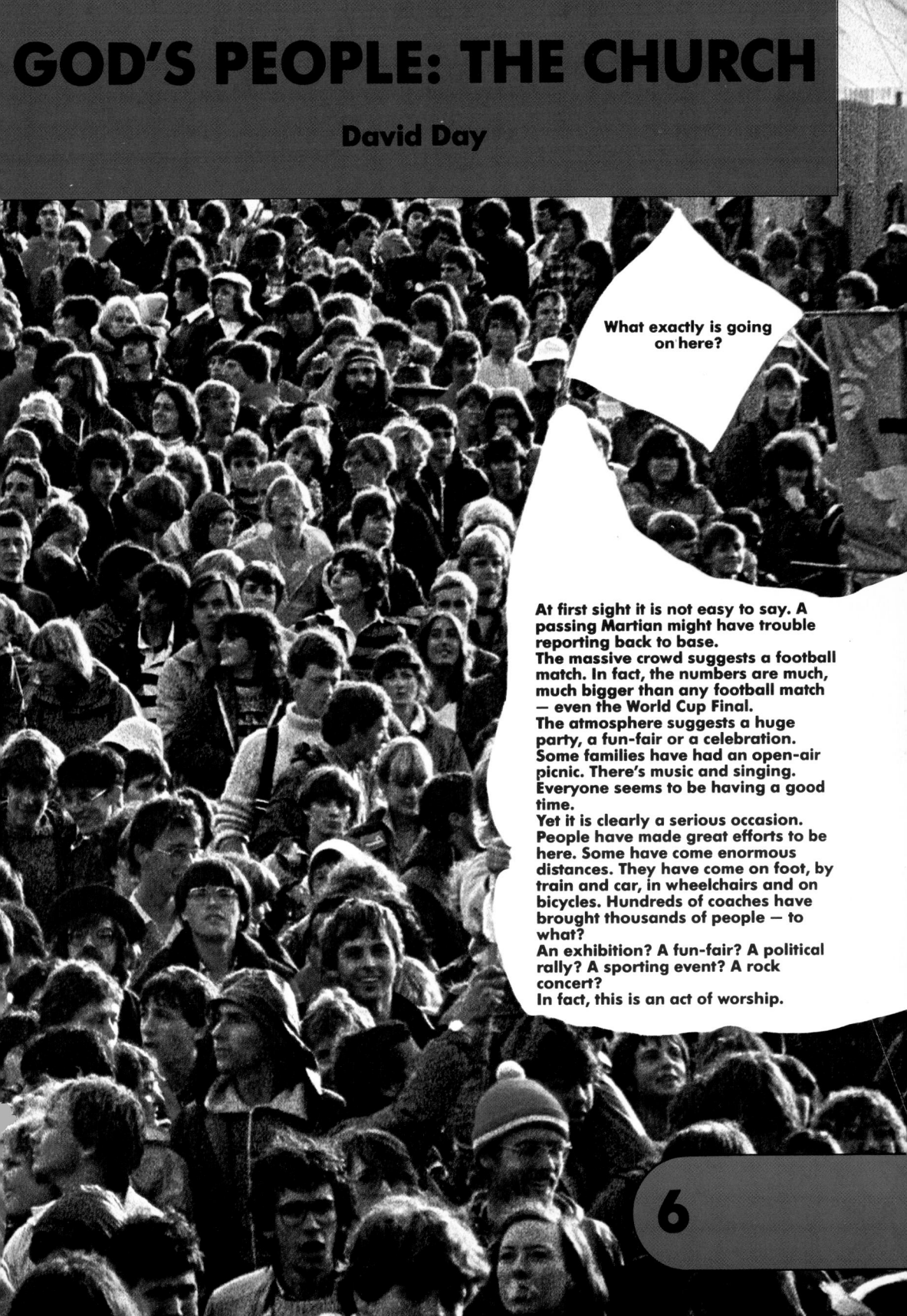

GOD'S PEOPLE: THE CHURCH

David Day

What exactly is going on here?

At first sight it is not easy to say. A passing Martian might have trouble reporting back to base.

The massive crowd suggests a football match. In fact, the numbers are much, much bigger than any football match — even the World Cup Final.

The atmosphere suggests a huge party, a fun-fair or a celebration. Some families have had an open-air picnic. There's music and singing. Everyone seems to be having a good time.

Yet it is clearly a serious occasion. People have made great efforts to be here. Some have come enormous distances. They have come on foot, by train and car, in wheelchairs and on bicycles. Hundreds of coaches have brought thousands of people — to what?

An exhibition? A fun-fair? A political rally? A sporting event? A rock concert?

In fact, this is an act of worship.

6

6.1 WHY WORSHIP?

'You have made me for yourself, O Lord, and our hearts are restless until they find rest in You.'
Augustine

Worship may seem a strange way to spend your time. What is it? Why would anyone want to do it?

Part of the answer is that it is human nature to worship. Even people who are not religious will worship a country, a cause, an idea or a hero. Everything else means nothing. The cause is bigger than they are. The hero is 'fantastic'.

Christians feel this way about God. He is 'bigger' than they are. He is awe-inspiring and 'fantastic'.

In one way, then, it does not make sense to ask *why* people worship God. They just do. It is natural. They can't help themselves.

Yet, even so, different people will stress different sides to worship:

● One man may just want to escape from the rat-race and find a still point in a crazy world.

● Another will be bubbling over with joy and excitement at what God means to him.

● A couple may want to say 'thank you' for the birth of a baby

● Someone facing a crisis will be hoping to see the problem in a new light.

● A family in mourning will look for comfort and strength.

● Someone weighed down with guilty feelings may come to receive God's forgiveness.

Sometimes, however, people come to church feeling that God is far away. One writer has called this 'the dark night of the soul' and it seems to be a normal part of experience. At times like this, worshipping is not an easy thing to do and the Christian has to hold on to God in spite of his doubts.

The heart of worship

For most Christians, the most important part of worship is the act of 'communion', the sharing of bread and wine.

It is special because Jesus himself set it up on the night before he died. At one level he was just holding a simple meal with his followers. There was nothing complicated about it. But the disciples would have had other thoughts in their minds as well:
● In those days a common picture of heaven was a feast, with the Messiah as host. So their thoughts would have turned towards Jesus as Messiah in God's kingdom.
● The meal was like all those other meals which Jesus had attended up and down Palestine. Everyone had been welcome at these. No one, however bad, had ever been sent away.
● But this meal was specially important. It was Passover. This festival was about freedom from slavery. Jesus was saying that he was the person who would set them free from sin.

The heart of the communion service has not changed. It is still like a meal. Someone takes bread and breaks it — as Jesus' body was broken on the cross. Wine is used to represent his blood poured out in death. The worshippers will eat and drink just as Jesus did.

What is the meaning of the communion? A service as profound as this has many meanings.
● Christians **remember and act out** Jesus' death on the cross for them. They share in the forgiveness the death of Jesus brings, and the new life of the resurrection.
● They **declare** the fact that they are one with him and that they intend to live their lives in the strength he gives them. Jesus is

'food and drink' to them.
● They also **look forward** to the day when the whole world will recognize that Jesus is Lord. One hymn calls the service 'a feast of victory', and this suggests the triumph of God over evil.
● They **share** in one meal. Christians remember that Jesus has accepted them all, even though they are not especially good people. So they ought to accept one another. They are brothers and sisters to all other Christians throughout the world.

To follow up more ideas on the communion service, see Section 3, **The Easter Faith**.

Christians all over the world remember the death of Jesus by sharing bread and wine together. Whether this is done in an Indian village (top) or a Western town (bottom), the heart of the service is the same.

What do people do in church?

Worship in church gives Christians a chance to meet each other and share their faith, to praise and thank God, to ask for his help, to listen to what he has to say to them and to make new decisions about how they ought to live.

In a church service Christians may:
kneel to pray
stand to declare what they believe and
    to sing hymns
sit to listen to readings and sermons
make the sign of the cross
raise their arms in praise
put their hands together
close their eyes
shake hands during 'The Peace'
put money in the offering plate

Most of these actions 'feel' right to the worshipper. For example, kneeling suggests that God is majestic. Closing the eyes is a way of concentrating on God and shutting out distractions. Shaking hands is a sign of friendship.

The exuberance and joy of these Nigerian worshippers leads them to dance in church.

Left The formality and solemn of some types of worship tell about the worshippers' view God.

These people raise their arms in worship to show their openness to God.

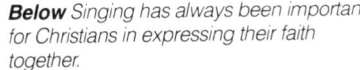

Below *Singing has always been important for Christians in expressing their faith together.*

Styles of worship

In some churches, most of the service will be led by a clergyman — someone specially set apart to do it. A set form of worship may be followed. In other churches the congregation will take a more direct part. People may pray aloud to express their own feelings to God. There may be dancing and hand-clapping and a series of mini-sermons.

The Society of Friends (or Quakers) concentrates on long periods of silence, while the Salvation Army is well-known for its cheerful band music.

Some services will emphasize the mystery of God. There will be solemn ritual, burning of incense, special robes and a formal dignified atmosphere. Others stress that God is found in the everyday — a deliberate attempt may be made to keep the service simple and informal. The language will be modern and the leader will probably wear ordinary clothes.

There is nothing wrong with this variety. Each style of worship points to a different part of the truth about God.

Above *An Indian family kneel together to pray. Kneeling in this way expresses submission and humility before God.*

Right *Many churches use a 'liturgy' in their worship. This is a fixed form of words which the minister and congregation read.*

Christians do not have to worship in a church building. There have been Sunday services in prison cells, in public libraries, in boats and pubs, in the open air, on the beach and even in a carpet factory.

But most services take place in a church.

Buildings are like codes. They carry a hidden message. Think of a classroom — blackboard, a teacher's table, desks — probably all facing the front. The shape of the room and its furniture send out messages about what goes on inside. Again, in a supermarket the tins of food and the long shelves point towards the checkouts at the exit. No one would think it was a bedroom.

Church buildings also carry messages about what the builders thought was important about Christianity and what they believed about God.

It is helpful to ask:
- 'What does this shape tell me?'
- 'Which way do people face?'
- 'What is it that dominates the building?'
- 'What sort of materials have been used?'
- 'Is it light or dark?'

There is no right way to design a church. Different designers 'say' different things. For example, seats set out in a circle emphasize meeting and sharing. An arrangement where the clergy and communion table are separated from the people emphasizes mystery and holiness.

If expensive materials — stone, hardwood, stained glass — have been used, then they preach a message about the majesty of God, and the dedication of people's gifts. 'Only the best is good enough for God.'

Other buildings may carry a different message: of simplicity, or poverty, for instance: God's people are identifying themselves with the poor and weak and sinful.

This cathedral in Liverpool, England, looks like a crown or a launching pad. It seems to say, 'Christ is king' even in the space age.

A modern church with lots of concrete and steel says, 'God is interested in ordinary people. He knows about computers. He is a seven-day-a-week God.'

An ancient church with few windows suggests that God is awe-inspiring, mysterious and eternal.

Right John Wesley's chapel in Bristol, England. Notice the double-decker pulpit, for preaching and reading from the Bible. He put them in the centre because he wanted to stress the importance of Jesus' message to the world.

Below People gather for worship in a simple building made in the same way as their own homes. This emphasizes that we can meet to worship God without special buildings.

Below Durham Cathedral in England reminds Christians that God is like 'a mighty fortress'.

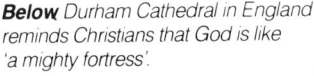

To think of the church as a lot of buildings is to miss the point.

The church is made up of *people* not bricks.

The New Testament does not seem to consider that someone can be a Christian on their own.

The word-pictures used in the Bible to describe the church make the same point.

● It is a **family**. This means that there is one Father and many brothers and sisters. Members of a family usually have a strong loyalty to one another.

● It is a **body**. Paul says that Jesus is like the head or brain and his followers are like limbs and organs. If one part of a body is in pain, the rest of the body feels it as well. Every part of the body is vital for complete health.

● It is a **building**. Jesus is the foundation. Christians are like stones of different shapes and sizes. God builds them together so that they all fit perfectly.

Down-to-earth love

Caring must be real, not just symbolic. Here are some cases of Christian caring.

One house in Cambridge is home for seven mentally handicapped people. Christians at a local church opened the house: the aim, the vicar says, is to have somewhere where 'mentally handicapped people can grow both as individuals and as Christians'.

For over twenty-five years the Langley House Trust has provided homes for men coming out of prison. General Secretary Anthony Richards says, 'Christian witness comes across by the way the staff carry out their work.'

Bob Holman was Professor of Social Administration at Bath University. In August 1976 he gave up that side of his work to live on a housing estate. Since then he has kept open house for any young person who wants to drop in. He has started a football team, opened a Community Centre and been a personal friend to dozens of people with every kind of problem.

Caring and worship

These ideas — of being loyal, caring for one another, and fitting in together — are often illustrated in worship.

For example, in some churches, the service will contain an act called *the peace*. The worshippers turn to one another, shake hands and say something like 'the peace of the Lord be with you'. It is a sign of family love.

Many churches have meetings for sharing, or 'fellowship', where this sense of belonging, as members of a family, can be expressed. Many also emphasize practical care for other members of the community, such as the handicapped, the old or unwell.

The Runaway Slave

In the first century, Onesimus, a slave in Colossae, ran away from his master Philemon. The penalty for this was death. While he was hiding in Rome he met Paul and became a Christian. Paul told him he ought to return home, and said he would write to Philemon begging him to receive Onesimus as a member of the family, not a slave. This letter is now part of the New Testament.

'I make a request to you on behalf of Onesimus, who is my own son in Christ. I am sending him back to you now and with him goes my heart . . . Now he is not just a slave but much more than a slave: he is a dear brother in Christ. Welcome him back just as you would welcome me.'
Letter to Philemon

This Roman slave badge reads: 'Seize me if I should try to escape and send me back to my master.'

Our world is full of barriers which divide people — young/old; black/white; rich/poor . . . The church as a community, a body or a family wants to try to break those barriers down because that is what Jesus calls them to do.

This is why Christians have been described as a 'third race'. This means that Christians shouldn't take sides. They try to bring people together. When Paul looked at the first-century church he said, 'Gone is the distinction between Jew and Greek, slave and free man, male and female — you are all one in Christ.'

Left The Berlin Wall separates communist East Germany from democratic West Germany with barbed wire, searchlights, guard dogs and armed sentries. The wall was put up overnight in 1961 by the East Germans to prevent refugees fleeing to the West.

Below The wall is decorated with wreaths at the spot where a refugee was shot dead.

Good news for the poor

In 1978 a young man went to Calcutta. These excerpts are from his letters home: 'God spoke to me some weeks ago . . . Now I have no shoes and only a few articles of Indian clothing, which themselves are worn out — please don't think I look a freak — I look the same as 90 per cent of the people. . .'
'God's words were sure, "I am your refuge, you must go and be with the poor". The canal is one of the poorest areas of Calcutta, where hundreds live and starve on its infected banks. It was closed last year and now the water lies motionless, black, stinking . . . Our little factory is in the middle of this and the whole area is infested with rats . . .'
'When I enter the churches with bare feet and a worn-out top I am no longer welcome . . .'
'A beggar woman came into the factory compound to steal some cow-dung for fuel . . . Her hair was dirty and dry and all her bones stuck awkwardly out . . . The worst thing was that the upper half of one lower leg was totally infected. It took about thirty minutes to clean her wound and remove all the poison during which she cried weakly with pain . . .'

Today's barriers

In the modern world the barriers are slightly different, but just as difficult to break down!

● The Third World is kept in poverty while the West continues to get rich.

● There is often hostility between countries on either side of the Iron Curtain, and sometimes between different nationalities.

● Education can create misunderstandings between people: those with little schooling mistrust the educated — but they in their turn despise the ignorant.

● In industry bosses and workers are often at war, and strikes are the result.

● Prejudice about the colour of a person's skin can lead to race riots.

● The women's lib movement began because the world seemed to give men an unfair advantage in life.

● In Northern Ireland two communities, one from the Catholic tradition, the other Protestant, find it almost impossible to live together without bloodshed.

● The term 'Generation Gap' shows that there is often tension between old and young.

Tensions over differences between peoples has erupted in race riots in many countries in the modern world.

Christians in action

Christians are not perfect. But with God's help they do struggle to break down these barriers.

When they are being true to Jesus they try to make sure that the church is a place where everyone is accepted and valued.

They also have a duty to work towards tearing down the barriers wherever they exist in the world outside.

Disputes over pay, hours, conditions and cutbacks in industry have often sharply divided workers and managers.

Don't give up

David Sheppard was a sportsman who became Bishop of Liverpool. He has spent most of his life working in and writing about the inner city.

'Here are some signs of God's presence which are to be seen in the most disadvantaged areas of Merseyside.

A youth leader being repeatedly let down but always coming back for more; church people and other volunteers regularly visiting the elderly and handicapped, whether or not they are thanked; breaking down of old barriers between Protestant and Catholic so that congregations as well as clergy start to know each other and join hands in a project; reconcilers who bear the anger from both sides in a dispute without giving up.'

One person's creed

Nick is a teenager. This is part of his creed.

'Everything that God does has a time. I've had experiences of looking back and I've thought "Hey, God, what are you doing?", and then I've realized that "Well, all right, you know best." Sometimes I've been extremely angry. I try to do everything in front of God's face without trying to hide my feelings from Him. It really depends how hard He's hitting.

'Jesus? As a person in front of me, perhaps. Or beside. To help me when I get stuck in the mire. So in that sense He certainly pulls me out, lifts me up, brushes me down and sets me on the right path again.'

Christians are people who believe together. By doing this they are able to strengthen and enrich each other's faith.

If the church is one family how can it be split into so many different denominations? There are three main streams — Protestant, Roman Catholic and Orthodox. There are smaller groups within these three main groups. Of course, the differences ought not to be exaggerated. Christians have a lot in common — and in a family you can have strong disagreements without breaking up.

Nevertheless, it would be silly to pretend that there are no deep divisions to be sorted out.

Creeds

Christians may disagree about many things but most of the denominations accept the great creeds of the church. The word 'creed' comes from a Latin word *(credo)* which means 'I believe'. It is a short statement of what a person or group thinks is really important in life.

No one likes to think of himself as a person without any strong beliefs, someone who can be pushed around by other people. If you never stand up for yourself, you are not much better than a cabbage. When someone makes a stand and declares his views on life, he is almost 'saying his creed'.

Many modern creeds appear in the form of slogans or chants. Even 'we are the champions' is a kind of creed.

But not any old view will count as a creed. Some of the things people believe are no more than *opinions*. No one cares about a belief like: 'I believe this is mushroom soup but it might be tomato.' A creed is a strongly-held *conviction*. It is something at the centre of your world. It is something you base your life on. It is, as people sometimes say, 'something you'd go to the stake for.'

How were creeds used?

It is not surprising that the first Christians wrote creeds. They used

these summaries of what they believed in at least two different ways:

● The creed gave the new Christian a chance to make a **public confession of his faith** in front of the whole church. The very best time for this was at a baptism service because this was the moment when a person 'crossed the line' and took the risk of becoming a Christian. The creed that was normally used was in the form of three questions and this creed still appears in some of the modern baptism services.

● Creeds were also used as **passwords** according to one early Christian writer. This is like what happens in wartime. Sentries demand the password for the day in order to know if someone is friend or foe. By the time Christianity had spread and got more complicated, creeds were used as a test to see if a person could be considered 'orthodox' (or 'right-thinking'). The creeds became like a fence. Some people

were inside; others were shut out.

Many of those who were shut out reckoned that they were the ones with the right belief and the rest were wrong. For centuries Christians tried to hammer out the best way of talking about God. This helped define beliefs.

Finding the words

This was very difficult. Human beings were trying to use words to describe what was beyond words.

It was like describing a spiral staircase without being allowed to use your hands. Or talking about the taste of new potatoes to someone who had never eaten them. Imagine a planet where there were no curved lines. How could an astronaut from earth explain to the inhabitants what a circle was?

Probably the biggest argument developed over the best way to describe Jesus Christ. The disagreement was so fierce that the Emperor Constantine called a council of church leaders at Nicea in AD 325.

Was Jesus really God? Or did God create him? But then he would be no more than a kind of super-angel.

The council decided that Christ was none other than God himself in human form. This was agreed by a later council held in Constantinople nearly sixty years later. It produced the most famous of all the creeds. Christians call it the Nicene Creed.

Common ground

Despite all the different opinions and arguments Christians have certain foundation beliefs which they all hold.

● This world is God's world even though it has gone wrong.

● Jesus is God's rescue operation.

What's the difference?

Here are some of the most important differences between the main Christian streams:

● **The authority of the Pope** is accepted by Roman Catholics but not by Protestants or Orthodox.

● **The Virgin Mary** is reverenced by Protestants as the mother of Jesus, but is not given the very special place she holds in the Roman church.

● **Baptism:** Many denominations like the Baptists and Brethren baptize only adults. Others like Anglicans and Methodists will baptize small babies. These are differences among only Protestant churches.

● Some branches of the church emphasize that **bishops and priests** are God's representatives in a special way. Others see every Christian as a priest.

● All Christians take **the Bible** seriously. But they disagree quite strongly on the question: 'How far should you take the Bible literally?'

● In the same way, all Christians take **worship** seriously. But they can be deeply divided about styles of worship. For example, Pentecostals emphasize that all Christians have a personal experience of the Holy Spirit and may contribute their individual gifts to a service.

'I sign you with the cross, the sign of Christ. Do not be ashamed to confess the faith of Christ crucified.'
Church of England Baptism service.

St Patrick's Breastplate

I bind this day to me for ever
By power of faith, Christ's
    incarnation
His baptism in the Jordan
    river
His death on cross for my
    salvation.
His bursting from the spiced
    tomb
His riding up the heavenly
    way
His coming at the day of
    doom
I bind unto myself today
St Patrick (AD 385-461), who
wrote this hymn, thought of
his faith as a breastplate to
protect him throughout his
life.

Three Questions

The three-question creed
from a baptismal service:
'Do you believe and trust in
    God the Father,
who made the world?'
'I believe and trust in him.'
'Do you believe and trust in
    his Son Jesus Christ,
who redeemed mankind?'
'I believe and trust in him.'
'Do you believe and trust in
    his Holy Spirit,
who gives life to the people
    of God?'
'I believe and trust in him.'

● Jesus lived, died and rose from the grave.
● The Holy Spirit is at work in those who claim Jesus is their Lord.
● The mistakes of the past can be blotted out.
● They can enjoy a new kind of living because they follow Jesus.

These basic ideas have been put in many different ways. The first creed was probably just 'Jesus is Lord'. The sign of a fish has been a shorthand creed for hundreds of years.

Witnesses and martyrs

One of the most moving modern statements of Christian belief is the Barmen Declaration. In 1934 some German Christians, calling themselves the 'Confessing Church', met at Barmen and set out in six points their opposition to the Nazis. It was not possible, they claimed, to have Adolf Hitler as leader as well as Jesus Christ.

The Confessing Church was taking a big risk. In fact, confessing the faith has often led Christians into trouble.

This has even affected the language we use. The Greek word for a witness is *martus*. From *martus* comes the English word 'martyr', which means someone who is killed for the faith. So many 'witnesses' died that 'witness' and 'martyr' came to mean the same thing.

Even today it is not always easy to own up to being a Christian in public. In many places a person would be laughed at. In some parts of the world it can lead to prison, beating up or even to death. These Christians are saying the creed not just with their mouths but with their lives, in the way they live.

Some Modern Creeds

'Everyone has the right to life, liberty and security of person.'
Article 3 of the *Universal Declaration of Human Rights*
'Black is beautiful.'
'Property is theft.'
'The child shall in all circumstances be among the first to receive protection and relief.'
from *Declaration of the rights of the child* adopted by the United Nations in 1959
'A woman's right to choose.'
'No nukes.'
'The only safe fast breeder is a rabbit.'

Pulling together

The World Council of Churches was founded in 1948 to bring the denominations together. At the meeting in Vancouver in 1983, 840 delegates attended from over 100 countries, representing 400 million Christians. The assembly has set up many projects to combat worldwide racism and oppression.

The badge of the World Council of Churches shows the church as a boat. The Cross of Christ is the mast. The ship has no rudder since the Spirit of God is meant to steer it over the sea of life.

Arguing it out

Two points of view were in conflict at the Council of Nicea.
- One was held by **Arius**, who said:
   'There was a time when the Son of God did not exist.'
   'The Son is a creature and a work.'
- His fiercest opponent was **Athanasius**:
   'Who does not see that the brightness cannot be separated from the light?'
   'If Christ is less than God, he cannot be our saviour.'
   In the end the Arians lost.

The Confessing Church

The meeting of some German Christians at Barmen took place against the background of Hitler's anti-Jewish laws. Jews were not allowed to hold office in the state or in the church. It was dangerous to protest but a German newspaper ran this story:
   'God said to his Son: "Will you not descend and come to the help of Germany?" He answered, "No, I have no right of entry any longer because of the anti-Jewish laws. Will *you* not go down?" God answered, "No, if I leave my throne for only a moment, Adolf Hitler will come and sit in it."'
   A few days later, the newspaper was banned.

Part of the Barmen Declaration . . .
   'Jesus Christ is the one Word of God which we have to hear and which we have to obey in life and death.
   'The church's commission is to deliver *to all men* the message of the free grace of God.
   'It is a false doctrine that the church can allow herself to be given *special leaders* with *supreme powers*.'

The fish

The Greek word for a *fish* is ichthus. This stands for

I esous	= Jesus
CH ristos	= Christ
TH eou	= God's
U ios	= Son
S oter	= Saviour

From the Nicene Creed:
'We believe in one Lord, Jesus Christ . . .
God from God, *Light* from Light,
True God from True God,
Begotten *not made*.
Of one Being with the Father.'
   Notice how careful the Council was to stop anyone saying that Christ was just something God had created.

6.6 MILESTONES

Everyone marks the special occasions in life in a special way. We throw a party or give presents. We have a photograph taken. We put on clothes we would not wear for every day. Even the food and drink is different. Few people have beans on toast at a wedding.

For Christians, God is involved in the whole of life. He is interested in the 'milestones', the occasions that mark the start of a new stage. He is there at the beginning and at the end — and at all the moments in between.

Birth

It is not surprising, then, that when a baby is born Christian parents want to recognize God's interest and concern in a public act, sharing the occasion with their church 'family'.

Some parents have the baby baptized. The child is 'washed' in water (though usually a few drops will do!) as a sign that God wants to wash away sin. The child will also be marked with the sign of the cross. This is to show that he belongs to Jesus Christ. The cross is like a badge. From now on the child is a soldier in Christ's army. The whole service also says 'God loves this child even though he is too young to realize it.'

Other parents prefer to save baptism till later but will still offer (or 'dedicate') the baby to God. This is partly an act of thanksgiving and partly a way of saying 'We want to let Jesus into our child's life from the very beginning.'

Of course, the sign can be without meaning. Parents might be doing all this out of habit or because other people do. They might even believe it is a piece of magic or works like vaccination against smallpox.

Churches that baptize babies include:
- Roman Catholic
- Greek Orthodox
- Anglican (Church of England)
- Methodist

Churches that prefer to baptize only adults:
- Baptist
- Christian Brethren
- Pentecostal (Assemblies of God)

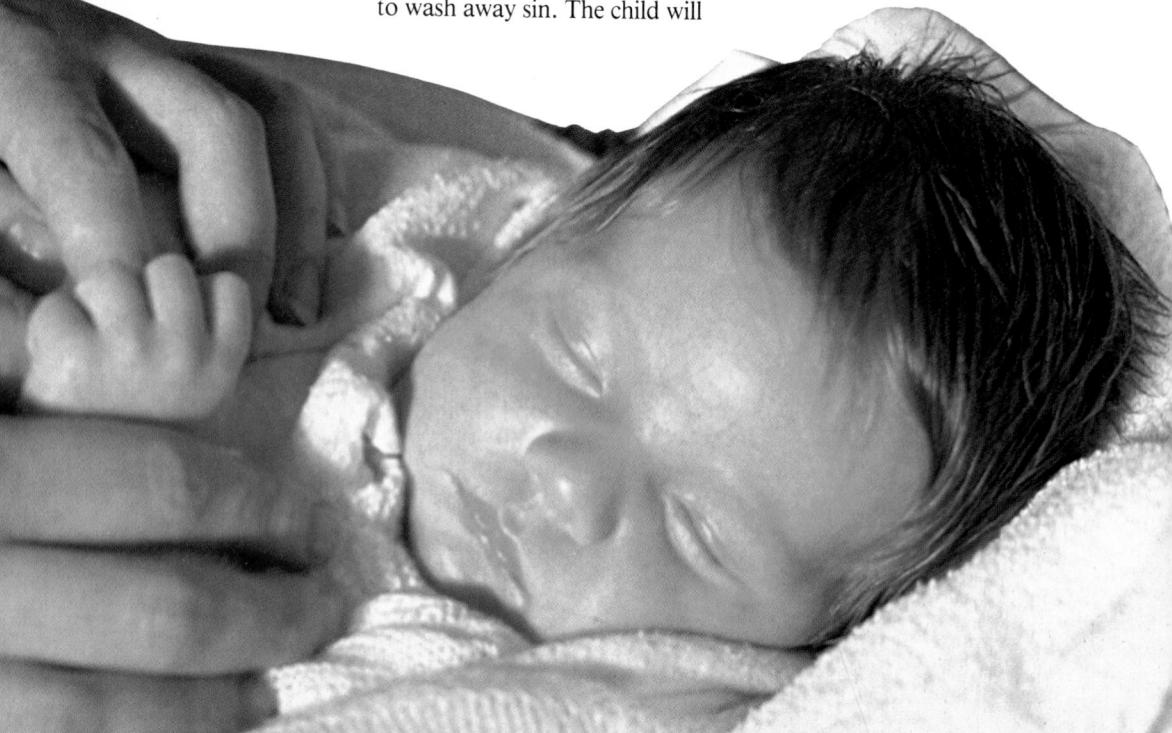

The arrival of a new baby is always a special event. Christians capture this special moment by baptizing or dedicating their babies to God.

A confirmation service in Africa.

Adulthood

Babies grow up — and some time during their teens young people have to sort out their own views on Christianity. Until then they have been riding on their parents' faith. Now they have to make up their own minds. This is a *personal* decision.

Many churches keep baptism for this moment. They think it makes better sense if the person who is baptized is making a personal confession of faith.

During the service a kind of death and resurrection will be acted out. People being baptized will be put completely under the water. It is as if they have drowned — their old life is 'buried' just as Jesus was. Then they are brought up out of the water as a sign of a new life. They have risen with Christ.

In other churches, confirmation plays the same part. Candidates publicly take on the promises which were made for them when they were children. They become *their* promises. Then the bishop will place his hands on the candidate's head as a sign of God's power coming into the person's life to help him or her to be loyal to those promises and to live like Jesus Christ.

People who want to be confirmed prepare for the event with confirmation classes, where they learn more about Christian belief.

The Marriage Vows

I, . . . , take you, . . . ,
to be my wife, (or husband)
to have and to hold
from this day forward;
for better, for worse,
for richer, for poorer,
in sickness and in health
to love and to cherish
till death us do part,
according to God's holy law
and this is my solemn vow.
I give you this ring
as a sign of our marriage.
With my body I honour you,
all that I am I give to you,
and all that I have I share
　with you,
within the love of God,
Father, Son, and Holy Spirit.

Marriage

Nobody has to get married in church. Every couple has a free choice.

But those who choose a church wedding are taking on the Christian view of marriage. This is different from other views in some important ways:

● The couple are deliberately asking God to bless their marriage and to be involved in every part of their life together. How they treat each other; how they bring up children; even how they spend their money — they will all be affected by what Jesus taught.

● The man and the woman make solemn promises to each other — not just in front of other people — but in the presence of God.

They promise to share every part of their lives, to act almost as one person, and stay totally faithful right up to death. Sharing every part of life includes the difficult times as well as the good times. This is one reason why couples pray for God's help. They recognize that marriage is not just a legal contract — and that romantic feelings will not be enough.

Why get married?

In recent years the Christian idea of marriage has been under attack. People are free, however, and perhaps a couple should not take on these promises if they do not intend to keep them.

One objection that is often made is that a wedding ceremony is just a pointless ritual that people go through because 'everyone else does it'. Some couples prefer just to live together.

In answer to this, Christians would point out the value and importance of a public act. It makes the relationship definite for the couple and it helps friends, neighbours and relations to understand that they must treat them differently from now on. In any case, people in love seem to *want* to declare that love and make public promises to one another.

A second objection is that Christian marriage restricts personal freedom. Those who say this argue that everybody changes. After ten years a couple might get bored with each other's company. They might not be able to get on together.

Choosing to love

One modern Christian leader defends the Christian view of marriage:

'My love for my wife is not blown back and forth by the winds of change, by circumstances and environmental influence. Even though my fickle emotions jump from one extreme to another, my commitment remains solidly anchored. I have *chosen* to love my wife.

Commitment is sorely missing in so many modern marriages. I love you, they seem to say, as long as I feel attracted to you — or as long as someone else doesn't look better — or as long as it is to my advantage to continue the relationship.

Sooner or later this unanchored love will certainly vaporize.'
Dr James Dobson

Against this, it can be argued that a marriage that is 'till death us do part' is the only kind that gives people security. Being able to trust the other partner takes away anxiety and fear; it gives a couple freedom to grow old without worrying about whether they are still attractive; it gives children a secure home in which to grow up; it gives someone time to grow as a person and get to know another human being at every level.

The happy couple pause to sign the register on their wedding day. Christian marriage means to make promises to each other before God, and to ask him to guide the marriage from day one.

Death

Death is such a solemn event that people have always surrounded it with special rituals.

For Christians, a funeral seems to have three purposes:

● It gives mourners a chance to pay their respect to the person who has died. The man who said 'They can tip me in the canal for all I care' was wrong. Funerals mark the fact that a real person has gone. They say 'This human life is precious'.

Left The rituals surrounding a funeral can be seen most clearly in a great state funeral, as here for President Kennedy, assassinated in 1963. The mixture of personal and national mourning can be seen in his wife and two children following the coffin, carried by members of the armed forces.

● It makes it clear that the person really is dead. This may seem a silly point but those who have lost someone they loved often will not admit it has happened. The service helps them to accept the truth, even though it is hard.

● It declares that because of Christ, the real person does not just rot in the grave. The hope of Christians is for a new kind of life with God.

It is impossible to imagine this and descriptions of heaven are obviously only pictures. Harps, crowns, white robes and pearly gates are not meant to be taken literally. But because Jesus is alive, Christians believe that death is not the last word. It is a comma, not a full stop.

Beginning and end

One title for Jesus in the Bible is Alpha and Omega (A and ß) — the first and the last letters of the Greek alphabet. The title seems to be saying that Jesus is like brackets. No part of life can fall outside his power and love.

Epitaphs

On a sailor:
This marks the wreck of Robert Woodward who sailed the seas for 55 years. When the Resurrection gun fires the wreck will be raised by the Angelic Salvage Company, surveyed and if found worthy, refitted and started on the voyage to eternity.
On a watchmender:
Died November 14 1802, aged 57.
Wound up in hopes of being taken in hand by his Maker, and of being thoroughly cleaned, repaired and set a-going in the world to come.

6.7 SPREADING THE NEWS

Christianity is a missionary religion — it goes out to people, and tries to convince them of its truth and persuade them to follow Jesus.

This is sometimes not a popular thing to do. Why not leave people alone? What right have Christians got to preach and push their religion? Who knows what the truth is anyway?

Christians do not see it this way. They believe they have 'good news' which they want to pass on and which others will want to hear. Indeed, Jesus commands them to tell other people the good news.

They are excited by what Jesus has done. Someone who supports a football team or who likes a pop group cannot help talking about

them. They go on and on. In the same way, those who believe Jesus has given them new life, has started a new world and set up a new kingdom, cannot stop themselves spreading the news.

One message, many messengers

Of course, there are many ways of being a 'witness' to Jesus Christ.
Christians try to point to him:
● by the sort of people they are;
● in the way they worship;
● by their concern for justice and freedom in society.

As well as this, however, they remember that Jesus told them to 'go into all the world and *preach* the good news'.

Preaching does not just mean speaking in a church, although that is one way. Evangelism (the word means 'spreading the good news') can take hundreds of different forms. For example:
● Church groups take to the streets: giving out leaflets, singing, speaking. Or groups of actors present the gospel in street drama.
● Some popular singers have put across the message about Jesus in gospel songs.
● International evangelists, like Billy Graham, preach at large open-air meetings. Billy Graham has done this for over thirty years and has been invited to dozens of countries. The meetings are often held in football stadiums to allow for the huge numbers which attend.

John Wesley

John Wesley, the founder of Methodism, spent fifty-two years of his life riding around Britain on horseback preaching the gospel.
● He got up at 4am every day.
● He covered 225,000 miles in his lifetime.
● He preached 40,000 sermons.
'I look upon all the world as my parish . . . in whatever part of it I am, I judge it right to declare unto all that are willing to hear the glad tidings of salvation.'

Billy Graham is said to have spoken to more people about Jesus Christ than anyone in history.

The pop singer Cliff Richard's music career started in the late 1950s. Since the mid-1960s he has been a committed Christian.

● Radio and television programmes can carry the Christian message.
● In many countries, processions and pilgrimages are held to celebrate Christian festivals or places connected with an act of God.
● Thousands of books, pamphlets, posters and badges are printed every year to communicate the Christian gospel.
● Teams of young people visit door-to-door, inviting people to meetings or giving literature.
● Evangelism can be seen in its most exciting form in the work of the missionary societies. Over the years, thousands of women and men have left their homes and gone

into a foreign country to translate the Bible, to build schools, hospitals and churches, and to teach and preach the good news.

Making up your mind

The purpose of all these different activities is the same. They are all intended to point people to Jesus — as the truth and the answer to mankind's problems.

They invite people to make a decision. In this they are copying Jesus' own example. Jesus' first disciples were fishermen from Lake Galilee. When he called them to follow him, they had to do something. They had to leave their boats behind and walk after him.

So Christianity has always said you cannot be a Christian by accident. A decision has to be made. When people make this

decision, turn their life round and take Jesus as their leader, the term 'conversion' is used to describe what has happened. A 'convert' is a new Christian.

This radio mast in the Seychelles broadcasts the Christian message worldwide.

Christians in action

There are hundreds of missionary societies in the world. The Missionary Aviation Fellowship is an unusual one. It was started in 1947 as a specialist service. It is not an airline but it does transport evangelists, pastors, missionaries, surgeons, doctors and nurses across mountains, jungles, swamps and deserts.

From Tanzania: Dr Janet Craven visiting villages in the bush, discovers a three-week-old baby seriously ill.

Mother and baby are flown back to hospital at Mvumi.

Late at night an emergency operation is performed.

The baby recovers and is named by the mother 'Nashukuru Ndege' — 'I thank the plane'.

As a teenager, Roy Catchpole went through courts and in and out of prisons. He was beaten up in his cell. He tasted utter despair. Finally he went to see the chaplain.

'Out of all my friends he was different . . . He said Jesus was still alive . . . and was around today. I didn't argue with him. He was dead serious. He said Jesus wanted me to be *his* prisoner.

'I looked at my hands which were torn and hard with callouses and cracks and cuts. I said, 'Jesus, if you want them, they're yours'.

'In the cold light of day I wished those things hadn't happened . . . It was an embarrassment.

'But I couldn't forget it.'

Roy Catchpole is now a Christian minister.

Christianity: growing or dying?

It is impossible to measure the number of new converts in each year. But the question is still an interesting one: Is the Christian church successful in its witness? Is Christianity growing or dying?

Of course, it isn't easy to say what 'successful' or 'growing' mean. A group could be small in number yet strong in faith. One or two individuals can sometimes have a wide influence. And the answers will be different in different parts of the world.

● Even **in the West** where Christianity sometimes seems to be weak, many more people go to a Christian church on Sunday than watch football on Saturday.

● In **Iron Curtain countries** the church is often persecuted and driven to hold its meetings in secret. This makes fact-finding difficult. Yet there is still a strong church, both meeting openly and as 'underground churches' meeting in secret. Even the Soviet authorities admit that 40 million people in the Soviet Union are still Christians.

Fact: Christians represent about a third of the world's population: 1,433 million out of 4,374 million (in 1980). Non-religious and atheists number about 911 million.

Fact: Christianity has now spread to 8,990 nations and is talked about in 7,010 languages.

● In recent years there has been a numbers explosion in **Africa and Latin America**. For example, the World Christian Encyclopaedia has calculated that Christians are increasing in Africa at the rate of 16,000 a day.

● In Hermosillo, **Mexico**, in one day over 3,500 people made a decision to follow Jesus Christ at an evangelistic crusade.

● In the Jotabeche church in Santiago, **Chile**, the orchestra numbers over 400, and the church building which seats 15,000 is full each Sunday.

● Probably the place where Christianity is growing fastest is in **South Korea**. A hundred years ago there were no churches at all. Now there are 3,000 in Seoul alone. One of these, the Full Gospel Central Church is the largest in the world, with a congregation adding up to 410,000.

From a worldwide viewpoint, Christianity seems to be growing.

The world's biggest church

'The Full Gospel Central church has seven consecutive back-to-back services — the first one beginning at 6.30 in the morning and the last one concluding at 8.30 in the evening. We were asked to attend the first service. There were 12,000 people in the auditorium when we arrived at 6 o'clock. If seats had not been reserved for us we would never have got in. Seoul is the only place on earth where there are constant Sunday traffic jams around churches.

After 2 hours there, we left the church just before the service closed. Ushers had to hold back rows of worshippers waiting to attend the second service. Do you know of any other place where people must wait in lines for Sunday services?'

The planet Saturn seen from the Voyager probe as it heads into deep space. In our age of scientific advance and technological revolution, the Christian faith can still speak to our deepest and most urgent needs.

History may just seem to be about people who lived hundreds of years ago. Their world was very unlike ours. There were no computers, motorbikes, videos or music-centres.

But Christians take the story of the church in the past very seriously indeed. Why?

● **Because God never changes.** 'History,' someone has said, 'is *his* story.' Christians look at what happened in the past as illustrations of the way God works in the world.

● **Because people don't change.** In some ways the lives of men and women in the past were totally different from ours. In other ways, human nature has not changed at all. Christians in earlier times were still people trying to serve Christ just as Christians do today.

● **Their story helps modern Christians to understand themselves and their world.** For example, they can see why Protestants and Catholics are divided — and can understand why there is such bitterness about in some parts of the world.

● **Church history also helps Christians to avoid the mistakes of the past** — people were burned at the stake in the name of Christ; the Inquisition used torture to deal

with those who seemed to be outside the orthodox faith; the Crusaders looted and killed while trying to reconquer Jerusalem from the Saracens — but winning back the Holy land is *not* the same as evangelism!

Not just history

Reading about the past is not just a history lesson for Christians. It shows them that Christianity is not a hobby or spare-time interest. It is a living faith that has lasted for nearly two thousand years. It demands everything a man or a woman has to give.

From history we learn that the power of Jesus shows itself in different ways. Each saint, martyr, missionary or reformer reflects some part of Christ's character. Nobody's life can do justice to the full range. Taken together, their stories illustrate what Peter called 'the multi-coloured grace of God'.

What do Christians feel when they read the history of the church?

Perhaps that the Christian faith is a treasure for which thousands have lived and died; that it has been handed on like a valuable object which has been in the family for centuries.

No Christian would like to feel that this story was going to end with him.

One New Testament writer put it this way:

'As for us, we have this large crowd of witnesses round us. So then . . . let us run with determination the race that lies before us.'

An inspired story

The history of Christianity is useful mainly to inspire and encourage twentieth-century Christians. It is full of saints and heroes, whose lives are a model or pattern.

Each great figure of the story illustrates a different truth about following Jesus and reflects a different aspect of what Jesus is like. To take just a few . . .

'Never, never will we desist till we have wiped away this scandal from the Christian name, released ourselves from the load of guilt and extinguished every trace of this bloody traffic.' William Wilberforce

● **William Wilberforce** (1759-1833) used his position in Parliament to fight the slave trade in Britain.

'I learnt how the sinner is declared "not guilty" by God's pure mercy by the way of faith — I felt myself born again as a new man and I entered by an open door into the very paradise of God.' Martin Luther

● **Martin Luther** (1483-1546) — the 'giant of the Reformation' rediscovered the truth that God accepts people freely, not because of what they have done, but because of what Jesus has done. No one need try to 'buy' his way into heaven.

'Death is the supreme festival on the road to freedom.' Dietrich Bonhoeffer

● **Dietrich Bonhoeffer** (1906-1945) was hanged by the Nazis for 'religious activities'. He was involved in the plot against Hitler and in smuggling Jews out of Germany. His life and death remind Christians of the cost of being a disciple.

● **Martin Luther King** (1929-1968) fought a similar battle in the United States to give black people their civil rights. Both men showed that Christ cares about justice and freedom for the oppressed.

'I have a dream that my four little children one day will live in a nation where they will not be judged by the colour of their skin, but by the content of their character.' Martin Luther King

'Take, Lord, all my liberty. Receive my memory, my understanding, and my whole will. Whatever I have and possess, thou hast given me; to thee I restore it wholly, and to thy will I utterly surrender it for my direction. Give me the love of thee only and I am rich enough; nor ask anything beside.' Saint Ignatius

● **Ignatius Loyola** (1491-1556) founded the Society of Jesus. This was (and is) an organization for those who wanted to serve Christ in total obedience. Their training was long and hard but they showed that being a Christian demanded full-time commitment.

'Lord, make me an instrument of thy peace: Where there is hatred, let me sow love; Where there is injury, pardon; Where there is doubt, faith; Where there is despair, hope; Where there is darkness, light; Where there is sadness, joy.' Saint Francis

● **Francis of Assisi** (1182-1226) was a rich young man who gave up everything to live a simple life. His poverty reminds Christians not to become slaves of money.